Pocket Crochet

18 Sweet Mini Amigurumi Companions

Tuva Publishing
www.tuvapublishing.com

Address Merkez Mah. Cavusbasi Cad. No 71
Cekmekoy - Istanbul 34782 / Türkiye
Tel +9 0216 642 62 62

Pocket Crochet

First Print 2025 / February

All Global Copyrights Belong to
Tuva Tekstil ve Yayıncılık Ltd.

Content Crochet

Editor in Chief Ayhan DEMİRPEHLİVAN

Project Editor Kader DEMİRPEHLİVAN

Designers Mei Li LEE

Technical Editor Leyla ARAS

Graphic Designers Ömer ALP, Abdullah BAYRAKÇI, Tarık TOKGÖZ, Yunus GÜLDOĞAN

Photography Tuva Publishing, Mei Li LEE

Illustrations Mei Li LEE

All rights are reserved. No part of this publication may be reproduced, stored in a retrieval system, or transmitted in any form or by any means, electronic, mechanical, photocopying, recording, or otherwise, without prior written consent of the publisher. The copyrights of the designs in this book are protected and may not be used for any commercial purpose.

ISBN 978-605-7834-89-8

 TuvaPublishing

INTRODUCTION

To my dearest friends, old and new, I am so happy to be meeting you again here in this wonderful new book!

It has been about two years since my second book, Amigurumi People, was published, and I am grateful that I have yet another new collection of patterns to share with you.

In the coming pages, you will be meeting 18 new adorable characters, who seemingly have nothing in common with each other (apart from the fact that they are all cute and about the same size!) Can you imagine a frog and a koala, a llama and a whale, or a penguin and a horse, enjoying the day together side-by-side?

Well, it is now possible in this little crochet world that we have designed for you and I'm really excited to see how you'll bring each contrasting personality to life.

Now, I wonder who you will be making first? I can't wait to see who will be your favorite.

Sending love and hugs and till we meet again!

PROJECT GALLERY

ROBERTA THE DINOSAUR
P.24

ROSIE LADYBIRD
P.28

PIPPEN THE PENGUIN
P.32

DUKE THE DOG
P.36

BESSIE THE COW
P.40

GINGER THE PONY
P.44

TABITHA THE GIRL
P.48

BARRY THE SHEEP
P.52

BILLIE THE BEE
P.56

LUCY THE LLAMA
P.60

MOTHER HEN & BABY CHICK
P.64

CHARLIE THE CAT
P.68

KELLY THE KOALA
P.72

PEPPER THE PUPPY
P.76

GRACIE THE GIRAFFE
P.80

BEATRICE THE BUNNY
P.84

FRANCIS THE FROG
P.88

WESLEY THE WHALE
P.92

CONTENTS

INTRODUCTION - 3
MATERIALS - 8
CROCHET TERMINOLOGY - 9
CROCHET BASICS - 10
GENERAL INFORMATION FOR MAKING
AMIGURUMI - 11
ADAPTING THE DESIGN - 12
SPECIAL CROCHET STITCHES - 12
SPECIAL EMBROIDERY STITCHES - 15
TIPS & TECHNIQUES - 16

PROJECTS

ROBERTA THE DINOSAUR - 24
ROSIE LADYBIRD - 28
PIPPEN THE PENGUIN - 32
DUKE THE DOG - 36
BESSIE THE COW - 40
GINGER THE PONY - 44
TABITHA THE GIRL - 48
BARRY THE SHEEP - 52
BILLIE THE BEE - 56
LUCY THE LLAMA - 60
MOTHER HEN & BABY CHICK - 64
CHARLIE THE CAT - 68
KELLY THE KOALA - 72
PEPPER THE PUPPY - 76
GRACIE THE GIRAFFE - 80
BEATRICE THE BUNNY - 84
FRANCIS THE FROG - 88
WESLEY THE WHALE - 92

MATERIALS & TOOLS

CROCHET & AMIGURUMI BASICS

MATERIALS

Yarn

HELLO Cotton Yarn is my latest go-to yarn of choice for making amigurumi. I really love the range of colors available and also how smoothly it slides on the hook without splitting.

Matte cotton yarns are my favorite, as it gives amigurumi an aged, vintage look that is so unique to handmade dolls.

PS It is perfectly fine to substitute the yarn used in this book with a yarn of your choice. Just remember to adjust the hook size accordingly.

Hooks

Indeed, not all hooks are made equal. Pairing your yarn with the right hook is absolutely necessary to make the amigurumi-making journey more enjoyable. I love the Clover Amour and also the Clover Soft Touch hooks, and I have one each in every size.

They are a good investment to make if you plan to crochet for a long time, as they can last for many years.

To know which hook size to pair with your yarn, try going one size smaller than the recommended hook size as shown on the yarn label. This will give you tighter stitches, and your amigurumi will be less likely to have "holes" with stuffing peeking through.

Hook Size Conversion Table

Metric	U.S.	UK/Canada
2.25 mm	B-1	13
2.75 mm	C-2	12
3.00 mm	-	11
3.25 mm	D-3	10
3.50 mm	E-4	-
3.75 mm	F-5	9
4.00 mm	G-6	8
4.50 mm	7	7
5.00 mm	H-8	6
5.50 mm	I-9	5
6.00 mm	J-10	4
6.50 mm	K-10 ½	3

Stuffing

Polyester fiberfill (also known as polyfill or fiberfill) is what I use for all my amigurumi. It is soft and fluffy and does not clump.

Good stuffing will give your amigurumi an even shape. I usually use the back of my Clover Amour hooks to push the stuffing in, especially for narrower pieces.

The Stitch Markers

When I first started crocheting, I didn't know about stitch markers and kept losing count of my rounds and had to start over multiple times. Locking stitch markers that don't fall out easily are absolutely necessary for beginners. A good substitute would be a safety pin or a paperclip.

Yarn Needle

This is one of the most important tools to have in your crochet bag as you will need to use it at least once during your amigurumi work, either to weave in ends or to sew different parts together. Find one that has an eye large enough to pass your yarn through. I use a blunt-tipped metal needle, but you can also try a bent-tip needle, or one made out of plastic.

Sewing Needle & Thread

I always keep a sewing needle and some thread in my crochet bag as you never know when you will need to use them for sewing on buttons and beads or strips of fabric.

Other Materials

Small scissors

Straight Pins

Mini Buttons

Beads

Jewelry Wire

Craft Glue

CROCHET TERMINOLOGY

This book uses US crochet terminology.

Basic Conversion Chart

US	UK
slip stitch (sl st)	slip stitch (sl st)
chain (ch)	chain (ch)
single crochet (sc)	double crochet (dc)
double crochet (dc)	treble crochet (tr)
half-double crochet (hdc)	half treble (htr)
treble (triple) crochet (tr)	double treble (dtr)

Abbreviations of the Basic Stitches

ch	Chain Stitch
sl st	Slip Stitch
sc	Single Crochet Stitch
hdc	Half-Double Crochet Stitch
dc	Double Crochet Stitch
tr	Treble (or Triple) Crochet Stitch

Standard Symbols Used in Patterns

[ ]	Work instructions within brackets as many times as directed
( )	Work instructions within parentheses in same stitch or space indicated
*	Repeat the instructions following the single asterisk as directed
**	1) Repeat instructions between asterisks as many times as directed; or 2) Repeat from a given set of instructions

Concise Action Terms

dec	Decrease (reduce by one or more stitches)
inc	Increase (add one or more stitches)
join	Join two stitches together, usually with a slip stitch. (Either to complete the end of a round or when introducing a new ball or color of yarn)
rep	Repeat (the previous marked instructions)
turn	Turn your crochet piece so you can work back for the next row/round
yo	Yarn over the hook. (Either to pull up a loop or to draw through the loops on hook)

CROCHET BASICS

Slip Knot

Almost every crochet project starts with a slip knot on the hook. This is not mentioned in any pattern – it is assumed.

To make a slip knot, form a loop with your yarn (the tail end hanging behind your loop); insert the hook through the loop, and pick up the ball end of the yarn. Draw yarn through loop. Keeping loop on hook, gently tug the tail end to tighten the knot. Tugging the ball end tightens the loop.

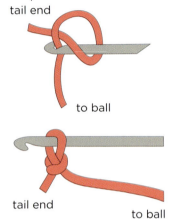

Yarn Over (yo)

This is a common practice, especially with the taller stitches. With a loop on your hook, wrap the yarn (attached to the ball) from back to front around the shaft of your hook.

Chain Stitch (ch)

The chain stitch is the foundation of most crochet projects. The foundation chain is a series of chain stitches in which you work the first row of stitches.

To make a chain stitch, you start with a slip knot (or loop) on the hook. Yarn over and pull the yarn through the loop on your hook (first chain stitch made). For more chain stitches, repeat: Yarn over, pull through loop on hook.

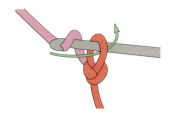

Hint Don't pull the stitches too tight, otherwise they will be difficult to work in. When counting chain stitches, do not count the slip knot, nor the loop on the hook. Only count the number of 'v's.

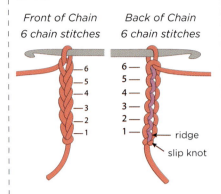

Front of Chain
6 chain stitches

Back of Chain
6 chain stitches

Slip Stitch (sl st)

Starting with a loop on your hook, insert hook in stitch or space specified and pull up a loop, pulling it through the loop on your hook as well.

The slip stitch is commonly used to attach new yarn and to join rounds.

Attaching a New Color or New Ball of Yarn or Joining with a Slip Stitch (join with sl st)

Make a slip knot with the new color (or yarn) and place loop on hook. Insert hook from front to back in the (usually) first stitch (unless specified otherwise). Yarn over and pull loop through stitch and loop on hook (slip stitch made).

Single Crochet (sc)

Starting with a loop on your hook, insert hook in stitch or space specified and draw up a loop (two loops on hook). Yarn over and pull yarn through both the loops on your hook (first sc made).

The height of a single crochet stitch is one chain high.

When working single crochet stitches into a foundation chain, begin the first single crochet in the second chain from the hook. The skipped chain stitch provides the height of the stitch.

At the beginning of a single crochet row or round, start by making one chain stitch (to get the height) and work the first single crochet stitch into first stitch.

Note: The one chain stitch is never counted as a single crochet stitch.

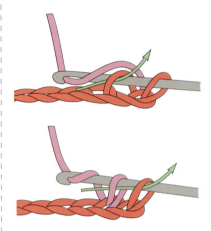

Half-Double Crochet (hdc)

Starting with a loop on your hook, yarn over hook before inserting hook in stitch or space specified and draw up a loop (three loops on hook). Yarn over and pull yarn through all three loops (first hdc made).

The height of a half-double crochet stitch is two chains high.

When working half-double crochet stitches into a foundation chain, begin the first stitch in the third chain from the hook. The two skipped chains provide the height. When starting a row or round with a half-double crochet stitch, make two chain stitches and work in the first stitch.

Note: The two chain stitches are never counted as a half-double stitch.

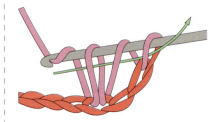

Double Crochet (dc)

Starting with a loop on your hook, yarn over hook before inserting hook in stitch or space specified and draw up a loop (three loops on hook). Yarn over and pull yarn through two loops (two loops remain on hook). Yarn over and pull yarn through remaining two loops on hook (first dc made).

The height of a double crochet stitch is three chains high.

When working double crochet stitches into a foundation chain, begin the first stitch in the fourth chain from the hook.

The three skipped chains count as the first double crochet stitch. When starting a row or round with a double crochet stitch, make three chain stitches (which count as the first double crochet), skip the first stitch (under the chains) and work a double crochet in the next (second) stitch. On the following row or round, when you work in the 'made' stitch, you will be working in the top chain (3rd chain stitch of the three chains).

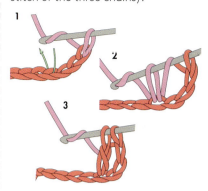

GENERAL INFORMATION FOR MAKING AMIGURUMI

Choosing the Hook

Use a hook which is a size or two smaller than what is recommended on the yarn label. The fabric created should be tight enough so that the stuffing does not show through the stitches.

Right Side vs Wrong Side of the Fabric

It is important to be able to distinguish between the 'right' (front) and 'wrong' (back) side of the crocheted fabric.

Right Side

Wrong Side

When working in a spiral or joined round, the right side of the fabric is always facing you. Working in rows or turned rounds, it will alternate between 'right' and 'wrong' side.

Single Crochet Rows

Working in a Spiral

Most of the amigurumi pieces are worked in a continuous spiral to create the dimensional shapes needed. Working in a spiral means that at the end of a round, you do not join (or close) with a slip stitch into the first stitch of the round. When you get to the end of the round, you start the next round by just working a stitch into the next stitch (which is the first stitch of the previous round).

Working in Joined (Closed) Rounds

Some parts of an amigurumi pattern might have 'joined rounds'. This is where, at the end of the round, you join with a slip stitch in the first stitch of the round. The next round starts with a number of chain stitches (based on height of the stitches used), and then you continue working stitches for the next round.

Note: Do not turn at the end of each joined round, unless instructed to do so.

Working in Rows

For some accessories or patches for your amigurumi, you will need to work in rows. Each row starts by turning the piece and working some chain stitches (known as the 'turning chain'). The number of chain stitches worked is based on the height of the stitches used.

ADAPTING THE DESIGN

There are many ways you can make your amigurumi toy unique.

Size By choosing a different weight yarn, you can make your toys either bigger (using thicker yarn) or smaller (using thinner yarn or thread). Remember to change your hook size too.

Colors This is the easiest way to make your toy unique. Select colors to match décor or personal preference.

Characteristics Changing the facial features of toys, gives them a whole new character. Adding (or removing) embellishments to the overall toy can change the whole look of it.

Eyes Changing the size or color of the eyes can create a totally different facial expression. Instead of using safety eyes, you can use buttons or beads for eyes. If there is a safety concern, you can sew on small bits of felt or embroider the features.

Appliqué patches Whether they are crocheted, fabric or felt (or a combination of these), adding appliqué patches to your doll is a great way to make your toys distinctive. They can be facial features, such as eyes, noses, mouths, cheeks, and maybe even ears. You can also make novelty appliqué patches to use as embellishment on the toys. For example – flowers on a dress, eye-patch for a pirate, overall patch for a farmer.

Embroidery By adding embroidery stitches to the face, (straight stitch, back stitch, etc.) or fancy ones (satin stitch, French knot, bullion stitch, etc.), your toy will take on a personality of its own. You can also use the cross-stitch technique to create a unique look.

Note: Embroider all facial features to make a child-safe toy.

Adding Accessories To create your one-of-a-kind toy, you can add various decorations to them. Colored buttons can be used in a variety of ways to spice things up. Using small ribbons and bows can feminize dolls. Attaching a small bunch of flowers or small basket to a doll's hand, tells a new story.

However you choose to give your toy character, each one ends up being unique!

SPECIAL CROCHET STITCHES

Single Crochet Decreases

a) Normal Single Crochet Decrease (dec)

1. Insert hook in specified stitch or space and pull up a loop (2 loops on hook).

2. Insert hook in following stitch or space and pull up a loop (3 loops on hook).

3. Yarn over and draw through all 3 loops on hook.

Single crochet decrease stitch made.

b) Invisible Single Crochet Decrease (inv-dec)

1. Insert hook under the front loop of each of the next 2 stitches.

2. Pull yarn through these two stitch loops (2 loops on hook).

3. Yarn over and draw through both loops on hook.

Invisible single crochet decrease stitch made.

Designer's Note: I usually use the invisible decrease when working in rounds, for a neater look.

Double Crochet Decrease (dc2tog)

1. Yarn over hook, insert into next stitch and pull up a loop. (3 loops on hook).

2. Yarn over and draw through 2 loops on hook (2 loops remain on hook).

3. Yarn over hook, insert into following stitch and pull up a loop (4 loops on hook).

4. Yarn over and draw through 2 loops on hook (3 loops remain on hook).

5. Yarn over and draw through remaining 3 loops on hook.

Double crochet decrease stitch made.

Treble Crochet (tr)

1. Yarn over hook twice, insert into next stitch and pull up a loop (4 loops on hook).

2. Yarn over and draw through first 2 loops on hook (3 loops remain on hook).

3. Yarn over and draw through 2 loops on hook (2 loops remain on hook).

4. Yarn over and draw through remaining 2 loops on hook.

Treble crochet stitch made.

Bobble Stitch (bob)

This decorative stitch creates a puffy bump on the surface of your amigurumi. It can be used to add texture on a piece of clothing.

1. Yarn over hook, insert into next stitch and pull up a loop (3 loops on hook).

2. Yarn over and draw through 2 loops on hook (2 loops remain on hook).

3. Yarn over hook, insert into same stitch and pull up a loop (4 loops on hook).

4. Yarn over and draw through 2 loops on hook (3 loops on hook).

5. Yarn over hook, insert into same stitch and pull up a loop (5 loops on hook).

6. Yarn over and draw through 2 loops on hook (4 loops on hook).

7. Yarn over hook, insert into same stitch and pull up a loop (6 loops on hook).

8. Yarn over and draw through 2 loops on hook (5 loops on hook).

9. Yarn over hook, insert into same stitch and pull up a loop (7 loops on hook).

10. Yarn over and draw through 2 loops on hook (6 loops on hook).

11. Yarn over and draw through remaining 6 loops on hook.

12. Chain 1 to secure.

Note: For the Small Bobble, repeat steps 1-8, ending with 5 loops on hook. Yarn over and draw through remaining 5 loops on hook, and chain 1 to secure and complete Small Bobble.

SPECIAL EMBROIDERY STITCHES

French Knot

This is a decorative embroidery stitch that I like using to create "dots" on a crochet piece, either for buttons or an animal nose.

1. Thread a strand of yarn through needle. Enter the crochet piece from the back to the front. Pull the yarn and needle out some ways from the piece. Wrap the working tail around the needle 3 or 4 times (depending on how thick you want your dot to be).

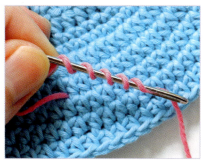

2. Push the loops together and while holding them in place, pass the needle through these loops and pull tight. A bump will form on your yarn strand.

3. Insert needle in the next stitch from front to back, making sure the Knot stays on the front. At the back, tie the ends in a knot to secure.

Back Stitch

Bring threaded needle up from wrong to right side of your amigurumi (#1). Insert needle back down (#2) and out again (#3). Then insert in same place where you came out (#1). Repeat according to the length required.

Straight Stitch

Bring threaded needle up from wrong to right side of your amigurumi, at the position you want to start the stitch (#1). Insert the needle back into the amigurumi at the position you want to end the stitch (#2). You may go over the same two positions several times to make a thicker straight stitch.

TIPS & TECHNIQUES

Double Magic Ring

The Double Magic Ring is a great technique to master. Whenever I crochet in rounds, I always start with a double magic ring as it leaves only a tiny gap once the ring is pulled closed.

A normal magic ring can also be used, but remember to secure the ring and weave in the tail after you have worked a few rounds.

1. Wrap the yarn tail twice around your finger.

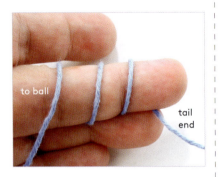

2. Insert the hook under the two loops and pull the working yarn through. Do not tighten up the ring.

3. Wrap the working yarn over the hook and draw the yarn through the loop on the hook. This secures the ring and does not count as a stitch.

4. Work the required stitches in Round 1 over both the loops into the ring.

5. When all the stitches are done, gently tug one of the loops (that formed the double loop on your finger) to close the ring.

6. Then tug on tail to tighten up the remaining loose loop. Round 1 worked in a Magic Ring is complete.

Working Around a Foundation Chain

This is ideal for making an oval piece I use it in the patterns throughout this book to make the shoes for each doll.

1. Chain the required amount of stitches called for in the pattern.

2. Starting in the second chain from the hook, work single crochet stitches in each chain across, but stop before working the last chain.

3. In the last chain, you make three single crochet stitches all in the same chain stitch, so that you end up on the other side of the foundation chain - instead of "turning" your work, you will be "rotating" to the other side.

4. Now you'll be working single crochet stitches in the other loops of the foundation chain across to the end. This will form the base - or Round 1 - of your oval piece.

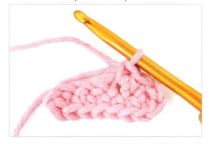

Changing Colors

When the pattern calls for a color change, you need to start changing colors in the stitch right before - the new color needs to be picked up in the final step before you complete the last stitch of the current color.

1. When you reach the last stitch before changing colors - make the stitch as you normally would until you have two loops remaining on the hook.

2. This is where you will pick up the new color and pull it through the remaining loops on the hook.

3. You can then continue crocheting in the new color.

Managing Yarn Tails in Color Changes

There are several ways to manage the yarn tail (of the old color) when you make a color change.

a) Cut and Tie Method

When you no longer need to go back to the old color, you can cut the old color and tie the old and new color tails together on the inside of your amigurumi piece.

b) Drop and Pick-up Method

When a pattern calls for alternating between colors at each round, and the color change happens at the start of every round, you don't have to cut the yarn of the previous color.

Just drop the old color to the inside of the work and then pick it up again when it is needed.

This will create a strand on the inside. Keep the strands slightly loose so the crochet piece does not pucker.

c) Carry-Along Method

This technique is very useful in patterns where a color change is used to create a special design on a piece.

Instead of cutting or dropping the yarn, you will "carry" the yarn along on the inside of the amigurumi piece (holding it together with the working yarn), as you make each stitch with the new color.

When it's time to change back to the old color, simply switch to the old color (which will now be the new color), and carry along the yarn from the previous color instead. You can do this back and forth until the color change is no longer needed.

Note: You may have to tug to tighten the yarn that is carried along frequently to make sure that the color doesn't show through on the right side of your amigurumi.

Fasten Off

At the end of your crochet work, you need to fasten off to ensure that your yarn does not unravel.

1. After the last stitch is made, cut the yarn, leaving a tail.

2. Yarn over hook and pull the yarn tail through the stitch. Tug to secure. This is how you "fasten off".

3. Keep the tail long for pieces that require sewing.

Needle Join (also known as Invisible Join)

This technique gives a clean finish to your pieces.

1. After the last stitch is made, cut the yarn and pull the tail through the stitch.

2. Thread the tail onto a yarn needle. Skip the next stitch and insert the needle under both loops of the following stitch. Pull yarn through.

3. Then insert the needle into the back loop of the last stitch made (the same stitch where the tail came through).

4. Pull the yarn gently so that it looks like a stitch and matches the size of the other stitches.

Close the Remaining Stitches

You can close the small hole made in the last round by using this method:

1. After fastening off, thread the yarn tail onto a needle.

2. Working in the last round of stitches, insert the needle in and out of all the front loops of each stitch around.

3. Pull the tail gently to close the center hole completely.

4. Usually at this point you secure with a knot or double stitch – before hiding the tail.

5. Insert needle back through the center hole into the stuffed piece and bring it back out on another side of your amigurumi.

6. Holding the tail taut, trim excess yarn.

7. The tail should disappear inside your piece.

Weave in Ends

When the yarn tail is no longer needed, you will need to "weave in ends".

1. Thread the yarn tail onto a needle.

2. Starting close to where the tail begins, working on the wrong side of your work, weave the tail through the back of the stitches.

3. Thread remaining tail ends inside your amigurumi to hide them. You can make a knot to ensure that they do not unravel. Trim excess.

Sewing Pieces Together

This step is usually the last step before completing your amigurumi, and one wrong move could ruin everything! Some things to remember:

1. A good habit to have is to pin the pieces in place first to check on their positions.

2. Make sure all the parts are facing the right way (head and limbs).

3. Hide unsightly jagged striped lines at the back, or on the underside of an arm.

a) Whipstitch

I use this stitch throughout, mostly to attach a "closed" piece to another "closed" piece (like an arm that is pinched close, attached onto the body).

1. With both pieces right-side facing, insert your needle through a crocheted stitch on the first piece, from front to back.

2. Bring the needle up through the corresponding stitch on the second piece, from back to front.

3. Insert your needle in the next stitch on the first piece from front to back. Repeat Steps 1 & 2.

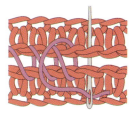

Mattress Stitch

This stitch creates an almost invisible seam when done neatly. I use this for attaching an "open" piece to a "closed" piece.

1. On the first piece, insert your needle in the same place where it came out and bring it up under the next stitch.

2. On the second piece, insert your needle in the same place where it came out and bring it up under the next stitch.

3. Repeat steps 1 & 2.

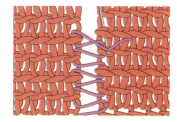

Stuffing Pieces

When it comes to stuffing your amigurumi, the more you stuff, the better your piece will hold its shape. Even a small tiny amigurumi may need quite a lot of stuffing, especially main body parts or legs which help a doll stand.

So, how do you know how much stuffing to use? Your doll should feel firm to the touch and not overly-squishy. But be careful not to over-stuff. You will know this has happened when you start to see stuffing peeking through your stitches.

When crocheting a piece that starts out with a smaller section (like a pair of legs that flows into the body), remember to start stuffing as you go along, or you may end up having a hard time trying to reach all the way into the amigurumi to fill all the parts up firmly. I like to use the back of my Clover Amour Hooks to push the stuffing in.

Surface Single Crochet

I use this often to add dimension to an amigurumi piece, usually for cuffs on pants and sleeves.

I also use it to make a foundation round when I need to crochet a piece of clothing that flows independently from the doll's body, like a skirt or a cardigan.

1. To start, make a slip knot on your hook. Insert hook into a stitch on your amigurumi piece from the front (right side) and out to a stitch next to it.

2. Yarn over and pull through both stitch holes. Now you will have 2 loops on the hook.

3. Yarn over and pull through both loops on the hook. Your first surface single crochet is made.

4. To make the next stitch, insert hook in the current stitch and out in the next stitch. Repeat instructions 2 and 3 above, until you have the number of stitches required.

Working in Front and Back Loops Only

Looking at crochet stitches, you can see a row of ">"s along the top. These are made up of **front** and **back loops**.

Unless otherwise instructed, all stitches are worked under both loops.

The front loop is the loop closest to you and the back loop is the loop furthest from you.

Working in **back loops** only creates a raised ridge on your piece.

This can be left alone for decorative purposes, or it can be used when working in the "unused front loops", which is useful for attaching on a new layer of work, for instance a skirt or a sleeve cuff.

Adding a Layer of Clothing

As they say, nice clothes can add to a personality. When crocheting directly onto the Doll, there are two ways you can try.

a) Working Round 1 with Surface Single Crochet

Using the Surface Single Crochet technique, work Round 1 directly onto the Body of the Doll.

1. Turn the Body of the Doll upside down. With a slipknot on your hook, make the first surface single crochet into any stitch (or as indicated) on the last round of the Body.

2. Continue to crochet all around. If you are making a skirt or a shirt, you will join the round with a slip stitch to the first stitch. If it's a coat or a cardigan, you will stop at the last stitch, make a chain and turn your work.

3. You can then continue on with the rest of the rounds, using Round 1 as your foundation round to build an independent layer of clothing from the Body.

b) Working Directly onto Unused Front Loops

Whenever you crochet in the **back loops** only, you create a series of unused front loops. These can be left alone as a decorative design. I like putting them to a better use by crocheting directly onto these front loops, usually to make a flowing skirt for the Doll.

1. Turn the Body of the Doll upside down. With a slipknot on your hook, make the first single crochet into any stitch (or as indicated) on the unused front loops on the Body.

2. Single crochet all around Body. Join the round with a slip stitch.

3. Continue with the rest of the rounds as instructed.

PROJECTS

Skill Level

★★☆
Intermediate

ROBERTA THE DINOSAUR

A little bit cheeky at times, Roberta is the friendliest dinosaur you'll ever meet.

Finished Size: About 4.9" (12.5 cm) tall

MATERIALS & TOOLS

HELLO COTTON YARN

Main colour (MC): Salmon (109) - for Head, Body, Arms, Legs, Cheeks and Tail

Colour A: Turquoise (134) for Spikes

Colour B: Cream (156) - for Muzzle

Colour C: Black (160) - for Eyes & Lips

HOOK SIZE
2.5 mm hook

OTHER
Toy Stuffing
Tapestry Needle
Stitch Marker

HEAD

Round 1: With MC, make a Magic Ring, 6 sc in ring. (6 sc)

Round 2: Inc in each st around. (12 sc)

Round 3: [Sc in next st, inc] 6 times. (18 sc)

Round 4: [Sc in next 2 sts, inc] 6 times. (24 sc)

Round 5: [Sc in next 3 sts, inc] 6 times. (30 sc)

Round 6: [Sc in next 4 sts, inc] 6 times. (36 sc)

Rounds 7-11: (5 rounds) Sc in each st around. (36 sc)

Round 12: [Sc in next 10 sts, inc in next 3 sts] 2 times, sc in next 10 sts. (42 sc)

Round 13: Sc in next 10 sts, inc in next 3 sts, sc in next 14 sts, inc in next 3 sts, sc in next 12 sts. (48 sc)

Rounds 14-16: (3 rounds) Sc in each st around. (48 sc) *(Image 1)*

Round 17: Sc in next 10 sts, [inv-dec] 3 times, sc in next 14 sts, [inv-dec] 3 times, sc in next 12 sts. (42 sc) *(Image 2)*

Round 18: Sc in next 9 sts, [inv-dec] 3 times, sc in next 9 sts, [inv-dec] 3 times, sc in next 12 sts. (36 sc)

Round 19: [Sc in next 4 sts, inv-dec] 6 times. (30 sc)

Round 20: [Sc in next 3 sts, inv-dec] 6 times. (24 sc)

Round 21: [Sc in next 2 sts, inv-dec] 6 times. (18 sc)

Start stuffing Head, adding more as you go.

Round 22: [Sc in next st, inv-dec] 6 times. (12 sc)

Round 23: [Inv-dec] 6 times. (6 sc)

Fasten off and close the opening securely. *(Image 3)* The front of the Head should have a flattened appearance. You can use your hands to gently squeeze and re-shape it.

MUZZLE

Round 1: With Color B, ch 10; starting in 2nd ch from hook, sc in next 8 ch, 3 sc in last ch, working on other side of starting chain, sc in next 7 ch, inc in last ch. (20 sc) *(Images 4 & 5)*

Round 2: Inc in first st, sc in next 8 sts, then leave the remaining sts unworked. (10 sc)

Clean fasten off and leave a long tail for sewing. *(Image 6)*

CHEEKS (Make 2)

Round 1: With MC, make a Magic Ring, 6 sc in ring. (6 sc)

Clean fasten off and leave a long tail for sewing.

BIG SPIKE

Round 1: With Color A, make a Magic Ring, 3 sc in ring. (3 sc)

Round 2: Inc in each st around. (6 sc)

Round 3: [Sc in next st, inc] 3 times. (9 sc)

Round 4: Sc in each st around. (9 sc)

Fasten off and leave a long tail for sewing. *(Image 7)*

SMALL SPIKES (Make 4)

Round 1: With Color A, make a Magic Ring, 3 sc in ring. (3 sc)

Round 2: Inc in each st around. (6 sc)

Fasten off and leave a long tail for sewing. *(Image 7)*

DESIGNING THE FACE

Sewing on the Muzzle

Sew Muzzle between Rounds 14-16 on the front of the Head. *(Image 8)*

Eyes

With Color C and a yarn needle, make 4 vertical straight stitches (one-stitch in height) for each Eye on Round 13. There should be 6 sts in between each eye. *(Image 9)*

Lips

1. To make the lips, you will need to split Color C up to thinner strands. Take 3 of the strands and use it to sew on a smile on the center of the Muzzle. *(Image 10)*

2. First, make a horizontal line, 3-sts in length, and bring the needle back up the centre of the smile and cinch the center with a stitch to secure the curve. *(Image 11)*

Sewing on the Cheeks

Sew on the Cheeks at each end of the Muzzle. *(Image 12)*

Sewing on the Spikes

1. Sew the Big Spike onto the top-center of the Head. *(Image 13)*

2. Position two Small Spikes framing the Big Spike and sew in place. *(Image 14)*

BODY

Round 1: With MC, make a Magic Ring, 6 sc in ring. (6 sc)

Round 2: Inc in each st around. (12 sc)

Round 3: [Sc in next st, inc] 6 times. (18 sc)

Round 4: [Sc in next 2 sts, inc] 6 times. (24 sc)

Rounds 5-9: *(5 rounds)* Sc in each st around. (24 sc)

Round 10: [Sc in next 2 sts, inv-dec] 6 times. (18 sc)

Fasten off and leave a long tail for sewing.

Stuff Body firmly.

ARMS (Make 2)

Round 1: With MC, make a Magic Ring, 7 sc in ring. (7 sc)

Rounds 2-4: *(3 rounds)* Sc in each st around. (7 sc)

Fasten off and leave a long tail for sewing. *(Image 15)*

FEET (Make 2)

Round 1: With MC, make a Magic Ring, 5 sc in ring. (5 sc)

Round 2: Inc in each st around. (10 sc)

Round 3: Sc in each st around. (10 sc)

Round 4: [Inv-dec] 5 times. (5 sc)

Fasten off and close the opening securely. Leave a long tail for sewing. *(Image 15)*

11CM HEIGHT

TAIL

Round 1: With MC, make a Magic Ring, 3 sc in ring. (3 sc)
Round 2: Inc in each st around. (6 sc)
Round 3: [Sc in next st, inc] 3 times. (9 sc)
Round 4: Sc in each st around. (9 sc)
Round 5: Inc in next 3 sts, sc in next 6 sts. (12 sc)
Rounds 6-10: *(5 rounds)* Sc in each st around. (12 sc)
Fasten off and leave a long tail for sewing. Flatten piece.

FINAL ASSEMBLY

1. Sew Body onto the Head. *(Image 16)*
2. Sew Arms onto the Body. *(Image 17)*
3. Sew Feet onto the lower part of the Body. *(Image 18)*
4. Sew two Small Spikes onto the upper side of the Tail. *(Image 19)*
5. Sew Tail to the back of the body - position it to the left side of the Body so that it will be visible from the front. *(Image 20)*

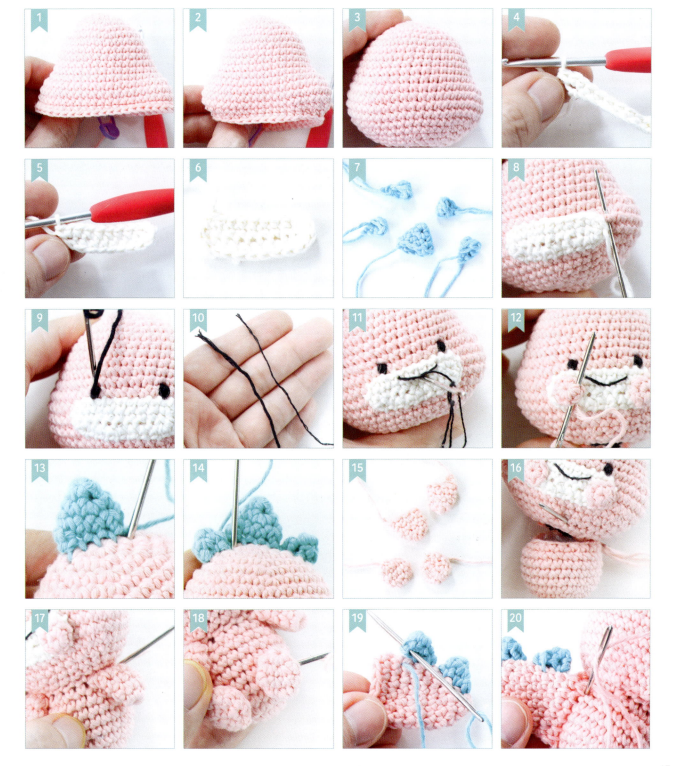

Skill Level

Intermediate

ROSIE LADYBIRD

Rosie is a sweet ladybird girl who loves showing off her spots.

Finished Size: About 4.9" (12.5 cm) tall

MATERIALS & TOOLS

HELLO COTTON YARN

Main colour (MC): Pale Peach (162) - for Head, Arms, and Legs

Colour A: Cherry Red (113) - for Hood, Body and Wings

Colour B: Blue (148) - for Hair

Colour C: Black (160) - for Face Details and Spots

HOOK SIZE
2.5 mm hook

OTHER
Toy Stuffing
Tapestry Needle
Stitch Marker

HEAD

Round 1: With MC, make a Magic Ring, 6 sc in ring. (6 sc)

Round 2: Inc in each st around. (12 sc)

Round 3: [Sc in next st, inc] 6 times. (18 sc)

Round 4: [Sc in next 2 sts, inc] 6 times. (24 sc)

Round 5: [Sc in next 3 sts, inc] 6 times. (30 sc)

Round 6: [Sc in next 4 sts, inc] 6 times. (36 sc)

Round 7: [Sc in next 5 sts, inc] 6 times. (42 sc)

Rounds 8-14: *(7 rounds)* Sc in each st around. (42 sc)

Round 15: [Sc in next 5 sts, inv-dec] 6 times. (36 sc)

Round 16: [Sc in next 4 sts, inv-dec] 6 times. (30 sc)

Round 17: [Sc in next 3 sts, inv-dec] 6 times. (24 sc)

Round 18: [Sc in next 2 sts, inv-dec] 6 times. (18 sc)
Start stuffing Head, adding more as you go.

Round 19: [Sc in next st, inv-dec] 6 times. (12 sc)

Round 20: [Inv-dec] 6 times. (6 sc)
Fasten off and close the opening securely. Leave a long tail for making eye indentations.

HAIR

Row 1: With Color B, ch 6, starting in 2nd ch from hook, sc in each st across. (5 sc)

Rows 2-3: *(2 rows)* Ch 1, turn, working in back loops only, sc in each st across. (5 sc)

Row 4: Ch 6, starting in 2nd ch from hook, sc in each st across. (5 sc)

Rows 5-6: *(2 rows)* Ch 1, turn, working in back loops only, sc in each st across. (5 sc)
Fasten off, leaving a long tail for sewing. *(Image 1)*

DESIGNING THE FACE

Making Eye Indentations

Using long tail on Head and yarn needle:

1. Bring needle up from base of Head and out to the left side of the head, positioning it at a stitch below Round 13. *(Image 2)*

2. Insert needle in next stitch, bringing it out at the base of the Head. Gently tug yarn to create a slight indentation. *(Images 3 & 4)*

3. Count 6 sts to the right, and repeat steps 1 & 2 to make another indentation for the other eye. *(Image 5)*

4. Secure yarn tail with a knot at base of Head and trim excess yarn.

Eyes

With Color C and a yarn needle, make 6 vertical straight stitches (one-stitch in height) for each Eye on Round 13. There should be 6 sts in between each eye. *(Image 6)*

Lips

1. To make the lips, you will need to split Color C up to thinner strands. Take 3 of the strands and use it to sew on a smile on Round 15. *(Image 7)*

2. First, make a horizontal line, 2-sts in length, and bring the needle back up the centre of the smile and cinch the center with a stitch to secure the curve. *(Image 8)*

Sewing on the Hair

1. Sew Hair onto the top part of the Head, on Rounds 7-10. *(Image 9)*

HOOD

Note: After Round 17, the Head needs to be placed in the Hood before continuing.

Round 1: With Color A, make a Magic Ring, 6 sc in ring. (6 sc)

Round 2: Inc in each st around. (12 sc)

Round 3: [Sc in next st, inc] 6 times. (18 sc)

Round 4: [Sc in next 2 sts, inc] 6 times. (24 sc)

Round 5: [Sc in next 3 sts, inc] 6 times. (30 sc)

Round 6: [Sc in next 4 sts, inc] 6 times. (36 sc)

Round 7: [Sc in next 5 sts, inc] 6 times. (42 sc)

Rounds 8-17: *(10 rounds)* Sc in each st around. (42 sc)

Place Head into Hood before continuing. *(Image 10)*

Round 18: [Sc in next 5 sts, inv-dec] 6 times. (36 sc) *(Image 11)*

Round 19: [Sc in next 4 sts, inv-dec] 6 times. (30 sc)

Clean fasten off and use tail to make several stitches all around the Hood to secure it to the Head.

FEELERS (Make 2)

Row 1: With Color A, ch 6, starting in 2nd ch from hook, 4 hdc in next ch, sl st in same ch, sl st in next 4 ch. (4 hdc, 5 sl st) Fasten off and leave a long tail for sewing. *(Image 12)*

BODY

Round 1: With Color A, make a Magic Ring, 6 sc in ring. (6 sc)

Round 2: Inc in each st around. (12 sc)

Round 3: [Sc in next st, inc] 6 times. (18 sc)

Round 4: [Sc in next 2 sts, inc] 6 times. (24 sc)

Rounds 5-9: *(5 rounds)* Sc in each st around. (24 sc)

Round 10: [Sc in next 2 sts, inv-dec] 6 times. (18 sc)

Fasten off and leave a long end for sewing.

Stuff Body firmly.

WINGS (Make 2)

Round 1: With Color A, make a Magic Ring, 6 sc in ring. (6 sc)

Round 2: Inc in each st around. (12 sc)

Round 3: [Sc in next st, inc] 6 times. (18 sc)

Rounds 4-9: *(6 rounds)* Sc in each st around. (18 sc)

Round 10: [Sc in next st, inv-dec] 6 times. (12 sc)

Round 11: [Inv-dec] 6 times. (6 sc)

Fasten off and leave a long end for sewing.

SPOTS (Make 4)

Round 1: With Color C, make a Magic Ring, 3 sc in ring. (3 sc) Clean fasten off and leave a long tail for sewing.

ARMS (Make 2)

Round 1: With MC, make a Magic Ring, 6 sc in ring. (6 sc)

Rounds 2-5: *(4 rounds)* Sc in each st around. (6 sc)

Fasten off and leave a long end for sewing.

LEGS (Make 2)

Round 1: With MC, make a Magic Ring, 6 sc in ring. (6 sc)

Rounds 2-3: *(2 rounds)* Sc in each st around. (6 sc)

Fasten off and leave a long end for sewing.

FINAL ASSEMBLY

1. Sew Feelers onto the top of the Hood/Head. *(Image 13)*

2. Sew Body onto the Head. Add more stuffing as you go. *(Image 14)*

3. Sew two dots onto the front of the Body. *(Image 15)*

4. Sew Arms to the sides of the Body. *(Image 16)*

5. Sew Legs at the bottom of the Body. *(Image 17)*

6. Sew one Spot on each Wing.

7. Sew Wings onto the back of the Body. *(Image 18)*

8. Optional: With a cotton bud tip and make-up blusher, add a pop of pink onto the cheeks for extra cuteness.

12CM HEIGHT

Skill Level

Intermediate

PIPPEN THE PENGUIN

This cute little penguin is extremely shy and secretly wishes that he could fly!

Finished Size: About 3.3" (8.5 cm) tall

MATERIALS & TOOLS

HELLO COTTON YARN

- **Main colour (MC):** Black (160) – for Head and Face Details
- **Colour A:** Light Grey (175) – for Body and Wings
- **Colour B:** White (154) – for Face
- **Colour C:** Nectarine (115) – for Beak and Feet

HOOK SIZE
2.5 mm hook

OTHER
Toy Stuffing
Tapestry Needle
Stitch Marker

HEAD/BODY

Note: When changing colors, carry along the main color yarn on the inside of the Head/Body. For the second color yarn, you may do the drop and pick-up method, which will create strands on the inside. Keep the strands slightly loose so the crochet piece does not pucker.

Round 1: With MC, make a Magic Ring, 6 sc in ring. (6 sc)

Round 2: Inc in each st around. (12 sc)

Round 3: [Sc in next st, inc] 6 times. (18 sc)

Round 4: [Sc in next 2 sts, inc] 6 times. (24 sc)

Round 5: [Sc in next 3 sts, inc] 6 times. (30 sc)

Round 6: [Sc in next 4 sts, inc] 6 times. (36 sc)

Round 7: [Sc in next 5 sts, inc] 6 times. (42 sc)

Rounds 8-9: *(2 rounds)* Sc in each st around. (42 sc) *(Image 1)*

Round 10: Sc in next 15 sts, change to Color B, sc in next 3 sts, change to MC, sc in next 5 sts, change to Color B, sc in next 3 sts, change to MC, sc in next 16 sts. (42 sc) *(Image 2)*

Round 11: Sc in next 13 sts, change to Color B, sc in next 6 sts, change to MC, sc in next 3 sts, change to Color B, sc in next 6 sts, change to MC, sc in next 14 sts. (42 sc) *(Image 3)*

Round 12: Sc in next 12 sts, change to Color B, sc in next 17 sts,

change to MC, sc in next 13 sts. (42 sc) *(Image 4)*

Round 13: Sc in next 12 sts, change to Color B, sc in next 18 sts, change to MC, sc in next 12 sts. (42 sc) *(Image 5)*

Round 14: Sc in next 12 sts, change to Color A, sc in next 18 sts, change to MC, sc in next 12 sts. (42 sc) *(Image 6)*

Round 15: Sc in next 12 sts, change to Color A, sc in next 18 sts, change to MC, sc in next 12 sts. (42 sc) *(Image 7)*

Rounds 16-20: *(5 rounds)* Change to Color A. Sc in each st around. (42 sc) *(Images 8 & 9)*

Round 21: [Sc in next 5 sts, inv-dec] 6 times. (36 sc)

Round 22: [Sc in next 4 sts, inv-dec] 6 times. (30 sc) *(Image 10)*

Round 23: [Sc in next 3 sts, inv-dec] 6 times. (24 sc)

Round 24: [Sc in next 2 sts, inv-dec] 6 times. (18 sc)

Start stuffing Head/Body, adding more as you go. *(Image 11)*

Round 25: [Sc in next st, inv-dec] 6 times. (12 sc)

Round 26: [Inv-dec] 6 times. (6 sc)

Fasten off and close the opening securely. *(Image 12)*

BEAK

Round 1: With Color C, make a Magic Ring, 5 sc in ring. (5 sc)

Fasten off and leave a long tail for sewing.

DESIGNING THE FACE

Sewing on the Beak

Sew Beak on Round 13 on the front of the Head. *Image 13)*

Eyes

With Color MC and a yarn needle, make 4 vertical straight stitches (one-stitch in height) for each Eye on Round 13. Position the Eyes about two-stitches away from each side of the Beak. *(Image 14)*

Eyebrows

With Color MC and a yarn needle, make 1 diagonal straight stitch (one-stitch in height) for each Eyebrow on Round 12, aligning it one-stitch away from each Eye. *(Image 15)*

WINGS (Make 2)

Round 1: With Color A, make a Magic Ring, 3 sc in ring. (3 sc)

Round 2: Inc in each st around. (6 sc)

Rounds 3-4: *(2 rounds)* Sc in each st around. (6 sc)

Fasten off and leave a long tail for sewing.

FEET (Make 2)

Round 1: With Color C, make a Magic Ring, 7 sc in ring. (7 sc) Fasten off and leave a long tail for sewing.

FINAL ASSEMBLY

1. Sew Wings onto Body, below Round 15. *(Images 16 & 17)*

2. Sew Feet onto the lower part of Body, between Rounds 19-20. *(Image 18)*

3. Optional: With a cotton bud tip and make-up blusher, add a pop of pink onto the cheeks for extra cuteness. *(Image 19)*

4. All done! *(Images 20-22)*.

Skill Level

Intermediate

DUKE THE DOG

This charming pup is always happy and loves a good joke.

Finished Size: About 4.9" (12.5 cm) tall

MATERIALS & TOOLS

HELLO COTTON YARN

Main colour (MC): Off-White (155) - for Head, Body, Arms, and Legs

Colour A: Black (160) - for Ear, Tail, Head Patch and Facial Details

Colour B: Russet (168) - for Ear

Colour C: Turquoise (134) - for Scarf

HOOK SIZE
2.5 mm hook

OTHER
Toy Stuffing
Tapestry Needle
Stitch Marker

HEAD

Round 1: With MC, make a Magic Ring, 6 sc in ring. (6 sc)

Round 2: Inc in each st around. (12 sc)

Round 3: [Sc in next st, inc] 6 times. (18 sc)

Round 4: [Sc in next 2 sts, inc] 6 times. (24 sc)

Round 5: [Sc in next 3 sts, inc] 6 times. (30 sc)

Round 6: [Sc in next 4 sts, inc] 3 times, sc in next 4 sts, change to Color A, inc in next st, change to MC, [sc in next 4 sts, inc] 2 times. (36 sc) *(Image 1)*

Round 7: Sc in next 22 sts, change to Color A, sc in next 3 sts, change to MC, sc in next 11 sts. (36 sc) *(Image 2)*

Rounds 8-10: *(3 rounds)* Sc in each st around. (36 sc)

Round 11: [Sc in next 10 sts, inc in next 3 sts] 2 times, sc in next 10 sts. (42 sc) *(Image 3)*

Round 12: Sc in next 10 sts, inc in next 3 sts, sc in next 14 sts, inc in next 3 sts, sc in next 12 sts. (48 sc)

Rounds 13-15: *(3 rounds)* Sc in each st around. (48 sc)

Round 16: Sc in next 10 sts, [inv-dec] 3 times, sc in next 14 sts, [inv-dec] 3 times, sc in next 12 sts. (42 sc) *(Image 4)*

Round 17: Sc in next 9 sts, [inv-dec] 3 times, sc in next 9 sts, [inv-dec] 3 times, sc in next 12 sts. (36 sc)

Round 18: [Sc in next 4 sts, inv-dec] 6 times. (30 sc)

Round 19: [Sc in next 3 sts, inv-dec] 6 times. (24 sc)

Round 20: [Sc in next 2 sts, inv-dec] 6 times. (18 sc)

Start stuffing Head, adding more as you go.

Round 21: [Sc in next st, inv-dec] 6 times. (12 sc)

Round 22: [Inv-dec] 6 times. (6 sc)

Fasten off and close the opening securely.

The front of the Head should have a flattened appearance. You can use your hands to gently squeeze and re-shape it.

EARS (Make 2 in different colors)

Round 1: With Color A/B, make a Magic Ring, 6 sc in ring. (6 sc)

Rounds 2-7: *(6 rounds)* Sc in each st around. (6 sc)

Fasten off and leave a long tail for sewing.

DESIGNING THE FACE

Nose

With Color A and a yarn needle, make one French knot (wrapping yarn 3 times around needle) centered on Round 11 of the Head. *(Images 5 & 6)*

Eyes

1. To make the Eyes, you will need to split Color A up to thinner strands. *(Image 7)*

2. Take 5 of the strands and use it to sew a pair of closed eyelids (diagonally) on Round 12 of the Head, about 2 stitches away from each side of the Nose. *(Image 8)*

Lips

1. With Color A (split yarn and use 5 strands only), sew a "W" shape with backstiches directly below the Nose, on Rounds 12 & 13 of the Head. *(Images 9 & 10)*

Sewing on the Ears

Sew Ears, one on each side, on Round 5 of the Head. *(Images 11 & 12)*

BODY

Round 1: With MC, make a Magic Ring, 6 sc in ring. (6 sc)

Round 2: Inc in each st around. (12 sc)

Round 3: [Sc in next st, inc] 6 times. (18 sc)

Round 4: [Sc in next 2 sts, inc] 6 times. (24 sc)

Rounds 5-9: *(5 rounds)* Sc in each st around. (24 sc)

Round 10: [Sc in next 2 sts, inv-dec] 6 times. (18 sc)

Fasten off and leave a long tail for sewing.

Stuff Body firmly.

ARMS (Make 2)

Round 1: With MC, make a Magic Ring, 7 sc in ring. (7 sc)

Rounds 2-4: *(3 rounds)* Sc in each st around. (7 sc)

Fasten off and leave a long tail for sewing. *(Image 13)*

FEET (Make 2)

Round 1: With MC, make a Magic Ring, 5 sc in ring. (5 sc)

Round 2: Inc in each st around. (10 sc)

Round 3: Sc in each st around. (10 sc)

Round 4: [Inv-dec] 5 times. (5 sc)

Fasten off and close the opening securely. Leave a long tail for sewing. *(Image 14)*

TAIL

Row 1: With Color A, ch 10; starting in 2nd ch from hook, sc in each ch across. (9 sc)

Fasten off and leave a long tail for sewing. *(Image 15)*

SCARF

Row 1: With Color C, ch 50.

Fasten off and knot the ends. Trim excess yarn. *(Image 16)*

FINAL ASSEMBLY

1. Sew Body onto the Head. *(Image 17)*

2. Sew Arms onto the Body. *(Image 18)*

3. Sew Feet onto the lower part of the Body. *(Image 19)*

4. Sew Tail to the back of the body. *(Image 20)*

5. Tie Scarf around the "neck" of the Body.

6. Optional: With a cotton bud tip and make-up blusher, add a pop of pink onto the cheeks for extra cuteness.

10CM HEIGHT

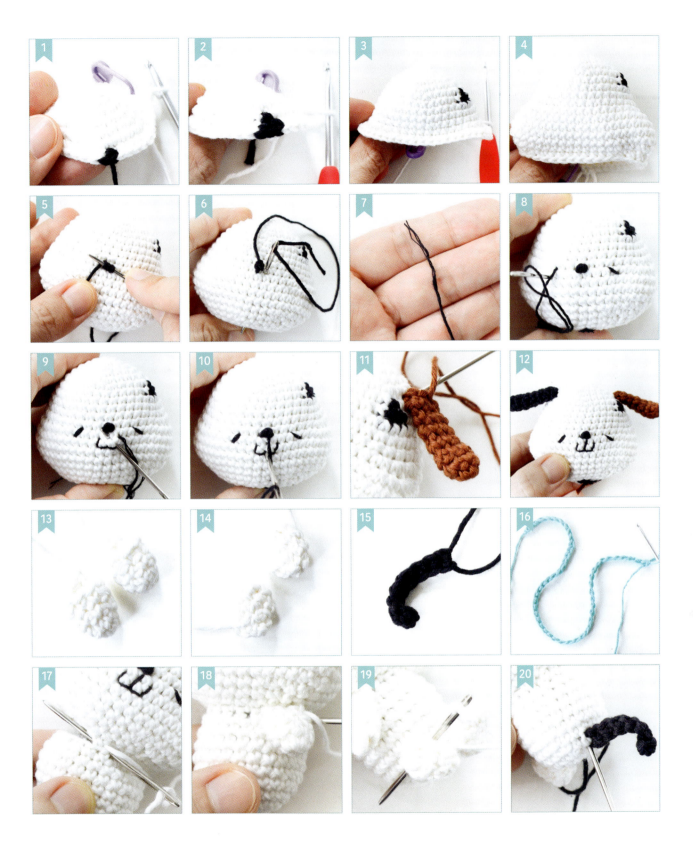

Skill Level

Intermediate

BESSIE THE COW

Bessie loves nothing more than to spend a day out with her friends in the field.

Finished Size: About 5.3" (13.5 cm) tall

MATERIALS & TOOLS

HELLO COTTON YARN

Main colour (MC): Off-White (155) - for Head, Ears, Horns, Body, Legs and Tail

Colour A: Black (160) - for Hoofs, Facial Details and Spots

Colour B: Pale Peach (162) - for Muzzle

Colour C: Turquoise (134) - for Flower

HOOK SIZE
2.5 mm hook

OTHER
Toy Stuffing
Tapestry Needle
Stitch Marker

HEAD

Round 1: With MC, make a Magic Ring, 6 sc in ring. (6 sc)

Round 2: Inc in each st around. (12 sc)

Round 3: [Sc in next st, inc] 6 times. (18 sc)

Round 4: [Sc in next 2 sts, inc] 6 times. (24 sc)

Round 5: [Sc in next 3 sts, inc] 6 times. (30 sc)

Round 6: [Sc in next 4 sts, inc] 6 times. (36 sc)

Rounds 7-11: *(5 rounds)* Sc in each st around. (36 sc)

Round 12: [Sc in next 10 sts, inc in next 3 sts] 2 times, sc in next 10 sts. (42 sc)

Round 13: Sc in next 10 sts, inc in next 3 sts, sc in next 14 sts, inc in next 3 sts, sc in next 12 sts. (48 sc)

Rounds 14-16: *(3 rounds)* Sc in each st around. (48 sc)

Round 17: Sc in next 10 sts, [inv-dec] 3 times, sc in next 14 sts, [inv-dec] 3 times, sc in next 12 sts. (42 sc)

Round 18: Sc in next 9 sts, [inv-dec] 3 times, sc in next 9 sts, [inv-dec] 3 times, sc in next 12 sts. (36 sc)

Round 19: [Sc in next 4 sts, inv-dec] 6 times. (30 sc)

Round 20: [Sc in next 3 sts, inv-dec] 6 times. (24 sc)

Round 21: [Sc in next 2 sts, inv-dec] 6 times. (18 sc)

Start stuffing Head, adding more as you go.

Round 22: [Sc in next st, inv-dec] 6 times. (12 sc)

Round 23: [Inv-dec] 6 times. (6 sc)

Fasten off and close the opening securely. *(Image 1)*

The front of the Head should have a flattened appearance. You can use your hands to gently squeeze and re-shape it. *(Image 2)*

EARS (Make 2)

Row 1: With MC, ch 7; starting in 2nd ch from hook, sc in next 2 ch, hdc in next ch, dc in next 3 ch. (2 sc, 1 hdc, 3 dc)

Row 2: Ch 1, turn. Dc in first st, dc in next 2 sts, hdc in next st, sc in next 2 sts. (3 dc, 1 hdc, 2 sc)

Row 3: Ch 1, turn. Sl st in first st, sc in next st, hdc in next st, dc in next 3 sts. (1 sl st, 1 sc, 1 hdc, 3 dc)

Fasten off and leave a long end for sewing. *(Image 3)*

For each Ear, gather the bottom part together and make several stitches to secure the shape. *(Image 4)*

HORNS (Make 2)

Round 1: With MC, make a Magic Ring, 3 sc in ring. (3 sc)

Round 2: Inc in each st around. (6 sc)

Fasten off and leave a long end for sewing.

MUZZLE

Round 1: With Color B, ch 10; starting in 2nd ch from hook, sc in next 8 ch, 3 sc in last ch, working on other side of starting chain, sc in next 7 ch, inc in last ch. (20 sc)

Round 2: Inc in first st, sc in next 8 sts, then leave remaining sts unworked. (10 sc)

Clean fasten off and leave a long end for sewing.

BODY

Round 1: With MC, make a Magic Ring, 6 sc in ring. (6 sc)

Round 2: Inc in each st around. (12 sc)

Round 3: [Sc in next st, inc] 6 times. (18 sc)

Round 4: [Sc in next 2 sts, inc] 6 times. (24 sc)

Round 5: [Sc in next 3 sts, inc] 6 times. (30 sc)

Rounds 6-15: *(10 rounds)* Sc in each st around. (30 sc)

Round 16: [Sc in next 3 sts, inv-dec] 6 times. (24 sc)

Round 17: [Sc in next 2 sts, inv-dec] 6 times. (18 sc)

Start stuffing Body, adding more as you go.

Round 18: [Sc in next st, inv-dec] 6 times. (12 sc)

Round 19: [Inv-dec] 6 times. (6 sc)

Fasten off and close the opening securely. Leave a long end for sewing. *(Image 5)*

BIG PATCH

Round 1: With Color A, make a Magic Ring, 9 sc in ring. (9 sc)

Clean fasten off and leave a long end for sewing.

SMALL PATCH (Make 2)

Round 1: With Color A, make a Magic Ring, 6 sc in ring. (6 sc)

Clean fasten off and leave a long end for sewing.

LEGS (Make 4)

Round 1: With Color A, make a Magic Ring, 7 sc in ring. (7 sc)

Round 2: Change to MC. Working in back loops only, sc in each st around. (7 sc)

Rounds 3-4: *(2 rounds)* Sc in each st around. (7 sc)

Fasten off and leave a long end for sewing. *(Image 6)*

FLOWER

Round 1: With Color C, make a Magic Ring, ch 2, dc, sl st into ring, [2 dc, sl st into ring] 4 times. *(Image 7)*

Pull to close ring. Fasten off and leave a long end for sewing.

TAIL

Row 1: With MC, ch 7; starting in 2nd ch from hook, sl st in next 6 ch. Fasten off and knot the yarn ends.

Split the strands of yarn to make a bushier tail. *(Image 8)*

Optional: Add glue to spread out and secure the shape of the tail.

DESIGNING THE FACE

Sewing on the Muzzle

Sew Muzzle between Rounds 13-16 on the front of the Head. *(Image 9)*

Eyes

With Color A and a yarn needle, make 8 vertical straight stitches (one-stitch in height) for each Eye on Round 11. There should be 6 sts in between each eye. *(Image 10)*

Nostrils

With Color A and a yarn needle, make 1 vertical straight stitch (two-stitches in height) for each Nostril on the Muzzle. Position them at the center of the Muzzle, with approximately 3-stitches between each Nostril. *(Image 11)*

Sewing on the Head Patch

Sew on a Small Patch to the front of the Head between Rounds 5-6.

Sewing on the Horns

Sew on the Horns on Round 3-4 of the Head, with approximately 5 sts in between each Horn. *(Image 12)*

Sewing on the Ears

Sew the Ears onto the sides of the Head, on Round 7.

Sewing on the Flower

Sew on the Flower to the right side of the Head, below the right Horn. *(Image 13)*

FINAL ASSEMBLY

1. Sew Body onto the Head. Make sure to position the Head to the right side of the Body, with the Body facing sideways, and the Head turned towards you. *(Image 14)*

2. Sew a Big Patch and a Small Patch on the left side of the body.

3. Sew Legs onto the bottom of the Body. *(Image 15)*

4. Attach the tail with a new strand of MC yarn. *(Image 16)*

5. Optional: With a cotton bud tip and make-up blusher, add a pop of pink onto the cheeks for extra cuteness.

12CM HEIGHT

Skill Level

Intermediate

GINGER THE PONY

Ginger loves apples and carrots and is always on the lookout for a sweet treat.

Finished Size: About 5.3" (13.5 cm) tall

MATERIALS & TOOLS

HELLO COTTON YARN

- **Main colour (MC):** Mocha (125) - for Head, Ears, Body and Legs
- **Colour A:** Russet (168) - for Bangs, Mane, Nostrils and Tail
- **Colour B:** Beige (157) - for Muzzle
- **Colour C:** Black (160) - for Eyes

HOOK SIZE
2.5 mm hook

OTHER
Toy Stuffing
Tapestry Needle
Stitch Marker

HEAD

Round 1: With MC, make a Magic Ring, 6 sc in ring. (6 sc)
Round 2: Inc in each st around. (12 sc)
Round 3: [Sc in next st, inc] 6 times. (18 sc)
Round 4: [Sc in next 2 sts, inc] 6 times. (24 sc)
Round 5: [Sc in next 3 sts, inc] 6 times. (30 sc)
Rounds 6-12: *(7 rounds)* Sc in each st around. (30 sc)
Round 13: Sc in next 9 sts, inc in next 3 sts, sc in next 6 sts, inc in next 3 sts, sc in next 9 sts. (36 sc)
Round 14: [Sc in next 10 sts, inc in next 3 sts] 2 times, sc in next 10 sts. (42 sc)
Rounds 15-17: *(3 rounds)* Sc in each st around. (42 sc)
Round 18: Sc in next 10 sts, [inv-dec] 3 times, sc in next 10 sts, [inv-dec] 3 times, sc in next 10 sts. (36 sc) *(Image 1)*
Round 19: Sc in next 9 sts, [inv-dec] 3 times, sc in next 6 sts, [inv-dec] 3 times, sc in next 9 sts. (30 sc)
Round 20: [Sc in next 3 sts, inv-dec] 6 times. (24 sc)
Round 21: [Sc in next 2 sts, inv-dec] 6 times. (18 sc)
Start stuffing Head, adding more as you go.
Round 22: [Sc in next st, inv-dec] 6 times. (12 sc)
Round 23: [Inv-dec] 6 times. (6 sc)
Fasten off and close the opening securely. *(Image 2)*

The front of the Head should have a flattened appearance. You can use your hands to gently squeeze and re-shape it.

EARS (Make 2)

Row 1: With MC, ch 5; starting in 2nd ch from hook, sl st in first ch, sc in next ch, hdc in next ch and dc in last ch. (1 sl st, 1 sc, 1 hdc & 1 dc)

Fasten off and leave a long tail for sewing.

MUZZLE

Round 1: With Color B, ch 10; starting in 2nd ch from hook, sc in next 8 ch, 3 sc in last ch, working on other side of starting chain, sc in next 7 ch, inc in last ch. (20 sc) *(Images 3-4)*

Round 2: Inc in first st, sc in next 8 sts, then leave the remaining sts unworked. (10 sc)

Clean fasten off and leave a long tail for sewing.

BANGS

First Strand: With Color A, ch 10, hdc in 2nd ch from hook, hdc in next 7 ch, (hdc, sl st) in last ch. (9 hdc & 1 sl st) *(Image 5)*

Next strand: *Ch 10, hdc in 2nd ch from hook, hdc in next 8 ch, sl st in same last ch on First Strand; repeat from * once more. (3 strands) *(Images 6-7)*

Fasten off and leave a long tail for sewing.

MANE

First Strand: With Color A, ch 30, hdc in 2nd ch from hook, hdc in next 27 ch, (hdc, sl st) in last ch. (29 hdc & 1 sl st)

Next strand: *Ch 30, hdc in 2nd ch from hook, hdc in next 28 ch, sl st in same last ch on First Strand; repeat from * once more. (3 strands)

Fasten off and leave a long tail for sewing. *(Image 8)*

DESIGNING THE FACE

Sewing on the Muzzle

Sew Muzzle between Rounds 15-17 on the front of the Head. *(Image 9)*

Eyes

With Color C and a yarn needle, make 6 vertical straight stitches (one-stitch in height) for each Eye on Round 13. There should be 5 sts in between each eye. *(Image 10)*

Nostrils

With Color A and a yarn needle, make 2 French knots (wrapping yarn 2 times around needle) on the Muzzle. There should be 5 sts in between each Nostril. *(Image 11)*

Sewing on the Ears

Sew the Ears onto the sides of the Head, on Rounds 2-3. *(Image 12)*

Sewing on the Bangs

Position the Bangs (wrong side up) in the area between the ears and sew to secure. With the wrong side up, the Bangs will naturally fall downwards towards the face. *(Image 13)*

Sewing on the Mane

1. Align the Mane (wrong side up) to the Bangs at the back of the Head. Make several stitches to the upper part of the Mane to secure the "roots" to the Head. Do not trim yarn ends yet. *(Image 14)*

2. Guide the strands of the mane to flow towards the left side of the Head. With the same yarn end, make several stitches to the mid-part of the Mane; this will keep the strands flowing to the left and visible from the front. *(Image 15)*

BODY

Round 1: With MC, make a Magic Ring, 6 sc in ring. (6 sc)

Round 2: Inc in each st around. (12 sc)

Round 3: [Sc in next st, inc] 6 times. (18 sc)

Round 4: [Sc in next 2 sts, inc] 6 times. (24 sc)

Rounds 5-14: *(10 rounds)* Sc in each st around. (24 sc)

Round 15: [Sc in next 2 sts, inv-dec] 6 times. (18 sc)

Start stuffing Body, adding more as you go.

Round 16: [Sc in next st, inv-dec] 6 times. (12 sc)

Round 17: [Inv-dec] 6 times. (6 sc)

Fasten off and close the opening securely. Leave a long tail for sewing.

LEGS (Make 4)

Round 1: With MC, make a Magic Ring, 7 sc in ring. (7 sc)

Round 2: Working in back loops only, sc in each st around. (7 sc)

Rounds 3-4: *(2 rounds)* Sc in each st around. (7 sc)

Fasten off and leave a long tail for sewing.

TAIL

Row 1: With Color A, ch 15, hdc in 2nd ch from hook, hdc in next 13 ch. (14 hdc)

Fasten off and leave a long tail for sewing.

FINAL ASSEMBLY

1. Sew Body onto the Head. Make sure to position the Head to the right side of the Body, with the Body facing sideways, and the Head turned towards you. *(Image 16)*

2. Sew Legs onto the bottom of the Body. *(Image 17)*

3. Sew tail onto the back end of the Body. *(Image 18)*

4. Optional: With a cotton bud tip and make-up blusher, add a pop of pink onto the cheeks for extra cuteness.

Skill Level

Intermediate

TABITHA THE GIRL

Tabitha is as mischievous as she looks and is never without her big orange bow.

Finished Size: About 4.7" (12 cm) tall

MATERIALS & TOOLS

HELLO COTTON YARN

Main colour (MC): Pale Peach (162) - for Head, Arms and Legs

Colour A: Nectarine (115) - for Hair, Bow and Dress

Colour B: Brown (126) - for Face Details and Bow Details

HOOK SIZE
2.5 mm hook

OTHER
Toy Stuffing

Tapestry Needle

Stitch Marker

HEAD

Round 1: With MC, make a Magic Ring, 6 sc in ring. (6 sc)

Round 2: Inc in each st around. (12 sc)

Round 3: [Sc in next st, inc] 6 times. (18 sc)

Round 4: [Sc in next 2 sts, inc] 6 times. (24 sc)

Round 5: [Sc in next 3 sts, inc] 6 times. (30 sc)

Round 6: [Sc in next 4 sts, inc] 6 times. (36 sc)

Round 7: [Sc in next 5 sts, inc] 6 times. (42 sc)

Rounds 8-14: *(7 rounds)* Sc in each st around. (42 sc)

Round 15: [Sc in next 5 sts, inv-dec] 6 times. (36 sc)

Round 16: [Sc in next 4 sts, inv-dec] 6 times. (30 sc)

Round 17: [Sc in next 3 sts, inv-dec] 6 times. (24 sc)

Round 18: [Sc in next 2 sts, inv-dec] 6 times. (18 sc)

Start stuffing Head, adding more as you go.

Round 19: [Sc in next st, inv-dec] 6 times. (12 sc)

Round 20: [Inv-dec] 6 times. (6 sc)

Fasten off and close the opening securely. Leave a long end for making eye indentations.

DESIGNING THE FACE

Making Eye Indentations

Using long tail on Head and yarn needle:

1. Bring needle up from base of Head and out to the left side of the head, positioning it at a stitch below Round 13. *(Image 1)*

2. Insert needle in next stitch, bringing it out at the base of the Head. Gently tug yarn to create a slight indentation. *(Images 2 & 3)*

3. Count 7 sts to the right, and repeat steps 1 & 2 to make another indentation for the other eye.

4. Secure yarn tail with a knot at base of Head and trim excess yarn.

Eyes

With Color B and yarn needle, make 8 vertical straight stitches (one-stitch in height) for each Eye on Round 13. There should be 7 sts in between each eye. *(Image 4)*

Lips

1. To make the lips, you will need to split Color B up to thinner strands. Take 3 of the strands and use it to sew on a smile on Round 15. *(Image 5)*

2. First, make a horizontal line, 3-sts in length, and bring the needle back up the centre of the smile and cinch the center with a stitch to secure the curve. *(Image 6)*

Eyebrows

With Color B and a yarn needle, sew on a diagonal stitch on Round 10 for the Eyebrows, positioning them above each Eye. *(Image 7)*

Sewing on the Hair

1. The Hair is sewn on using a series of vertical straight stitches, stemming from the top of the Head and down to the front, side and back, accordingly. This style of sewing is similar to the "satin stitch" used in embroidery.

2. Start by cutting a manageable length of Color A yarn. Thread it through a yarn needle and bring it up from the bottom of the Head through to the top of the Head. Now bring the yarn back down into the Head, approximately on Round 8 (for the bangs). *(Image 8)*

3. Bring the yarn back out from the top of the Head and go back and forth, moving to the stitches next to it, till you've covered the front part of the Head with Hair. *(Image 9)*

4. When bringing the yarn back out through the top of the Head, remember to move to a spot next to it after every few stitches. This is to ensure that you do not have a hard time pulling the yarn and needle out from the same spot as it starts to thicken with many strands of yarn.

5. Continue in the same manner for the sides of the Hair and also for the back. The longer Hair strands should end on Round 15 or 16 to create a "bob" hairstyle. *(Image 10)*

6. Trim excess yarn at the bottom of the Head once you are done with the Hair.

BOW

Round 1: With Color A, ch 8; starting in 2nd ch from hook, sc in next 6 ch, 3 sc in last ch, working on other side of starting chain, sc in next 6 ch. (15 sc) *(Image 11)*

Rounds 2-6: *(5 rounds)* Sc in each st around. (15 sc)

Round 7: [Inv-dec] 7 times, sc in last st. (8 sc) *(Image 12)*

Round 8: Inc in next 7 sts, sc in last st. (15 sc)

Rounds 9-13: *(5 rounds)* Sc in each st around. (15 sc)

Fasten off and whip stitch the ends close.

Thread the tail end through to the bottom-center and leave a long end for sewing.

BOW CENTER

Row 1: With Color A, ch 12.

Fasten off and leave a long end for sewing.

DESIGNING THE BOW

1. Sew Bow Center to the center of the Bow.

2. With Color B and yarn needle, make 3 small "X" stitches on each side of the Bow. *(Image 13)*

BODY

Round 1: With Color A, make a Magic Ring, 6 sc in ring. (6 sc)

Round 2: Inc in each st around. (12 sc)

Round 3: [Sc in next st, inc] 6 times. (18 sc)

Round 4: [Sc in next 2 sts, inc] 6 times. (24 sc)

Rounds 5-6: *(2 rounds)* Sc in each st around. (24 sc)

Round 7: Working in back loops only, sc in each st around. (24 sc)

Rounds 8-9: *(2 rounds)* Sc in each st around. (24 sc)

Round 10: [Sc in next 2 sts, inv-dec] 6 times. (18 sc)

Fasten off and leave a long end for sewing.

Stuff Body firmly.

SKIRT

Note: Round 1 is worked in the unused front loops of Round 6 on Body.

Round 1: Holding Body upside down, join Color A with standing sc to any st at center back, sc in next 24 sts; join with sl st to first sc. (25 sc)

Round 2: Ch 1, [hdc in next st, 2 hdc in next st] 12 times; join with sl st to first hdc. (36 hdc)

Fasten off and weave in ends.

ARMS (Make 2)

Round 1: With MC, make a Magic Ring, 6 sc in ring. (6 sc)

Rounds 2-5: *(4 rounds)* Sc in each st around. (6 sc)

Fasten off and leave a long end for sewing.

LEGS (Make 2)

Round 1: With MC, make a Magic Ring, 6 sc in ring. (6 sc)

Rounds 2-3: *(2 rounds)* Sc in each st around. (6 sc)

Fasten off and leave a long end for sewing.

FINAL ASSEMBLY

1. Sew Bow onto the top of the Head.

2. Sew Body onto the Head. Add more stuffing as you go. *(Image 14)*

3. Sew Arms to the sides of the Body. *(Image 15)*

4. Sew Legs at the bottom of the Body. *(Image 16)*

5. Optional: With a cotton bud tip and make-up blusher, add a pop of pink onto the cheeks for extra cuteness.

Skill Level

Intermediate

BARRY THE SHEEP

Barry has the softest wool and is the star of his flock.

Finished Size: About 5.3" (13.5 cm) tall

MATERIALS & TOOLS

HELLO COTTON YARN

- **Main colour (MC):** Black (160) - for Head, Muzzle, Ears and Legs
- **Colour A:** Light Grey (175) - for Hair, Body, Tail and Face Details
- **Colour B:** Blue (148) - for Eyes
- **Colour C:** Light Pink (102) - for Cheeks

HOOK SIZE

2.5 mm hook

OTHER

Toy Stuffing
Tapestry Needle
Stitch Marker

HEAD

Round 1: With MC, make a Magic Ring, 6 sc in ring. (6 sc)

Round 2: Inc in each st around. (12 sc)

Round 3: [Sc in next st, inc] 6 times. (18 sc)

Round 4: [Sc in next 2 sts, inc] 6 times. (24 sc)

Round 5: [Sc in next 3 sts, inc] 6 times. (30 sc)

Rounds 6-10: (5 rounds) Sc in each st around. (30 sc)

Round 11: Sc in next 9 sts, inc in next 3 sts, sc in next 6 sts, inc in next 3 sts, sc in next 9 sts. (36 sc)

Round 12: [Sc in next 10 sts, inc in next 3 sts] 2 times, sc in next 10 sts. (42 sc)

Rounds 13-15: (3 rounds) Sc in each st around. (42 sc)

Round 16: Sc in next 10 sts, [inv-dec] 3 times, sc in next 10 sts, [inv-dec] 3 times, sc in next 10 sts. (36 sc)

Round 17: Sc in next 9 sts, [inv-dec] 3 times, sc in next 6 sts, [inv-dec] 3 times, sc in next 9 sts. (30 sc)

Round 18: [Sc in next 3 sts, inv-dec] 6 times. (24 sc)

Round 19: [Sc in next 2 sts, inv-dec] 6 times. (18 sc)

Start stuffing Head, adding more as you go.

Round 20: [Sc in next st, inv-dec] 6 times. (12 sc)

Round 21: [Inv-dec] 6 times. (6 sc)

Fasten off and close the opening securely. The front of the Head should have a flattened appearance. You can use your hands to gently squeeze and re-shape it. *(Image 1)*

EARS (Make 2)

Row 1: With MC, ch 7; starting in 2nd ch from hook, sc in next 2 ch, hdc in next ch, dc in next 3 ch. (2 sc, 1 hdc, 3 dc)

Row 2: Ch 1, turn. Dc in first st, dc in next 2 sts, hdc in next st, sc in next 2 sts. (3 dc, 1 hdc, 2 sc)

Row 3: Ch 1, turn. Sl st in each st across. (6 sl st)

Fasten off and leave a long end for sewing.

For each Ear, gather the bottom part together and make several stitches to secure the shape. *(Image 2)*

CHEEKS (Make 2)

Round 1: With Color C, make a Magic Ring, 6 sc in ring. (6 sc)

Clean fasten off and leave a long end for sewing.

HAIR

Round 1: With Color A, make a Magic Ring, 6 sc in ring; join with a sl st to first sc (6 sc)

Round 2: Ch 2, [bob, hdc] in each st around; join with sl st to first bobble. (6 bobble sts & 6 hdc) Join all bobble-rounds in this manner. *(Images 3 & 4)*

Round 3: Ch 1, inc in each st around; join with sl st to first sc. (24 sc) Join all sc-rounds in this manner.

Round 4: Ch 2, [bob in next st, hdc in next st] 12 times; join (12 bobble sts & 12 hdc)

Round 5: Ch 1, [sc in each of next 3 sts, inc in next st] 6 times; join. (30 sc)

Round 6: Ch 2, [bob in next st, hdc in next st] 15 times; join. (15 bobble sts & 15 hdc)

Fasten off and leave a long end for sewing. *(Image 5)*

MUZZLE

Round 1: With MC, ch 10; starting in 2nd ch from hook, sc in next 8 ch, 3 sc in last ch, working on other side of starting chain, sc in next 7 ch, inc in last ch. (20 sc)

Round 2: Inc in first st, sc in next 8 sts, inc in next 2 sts, sc in next 8 sts, inc in last st. (24 sc)

Clean fasten off and leave a long end for sewing.

(Image 6)

BODY

Round 1: With Color A, make a Magic Ring, 6 sc in ring. (6 sc)

Round 2: Inc in each st around. (12 sc)

Round 3: [Sc in next st, inc] 6 times. (18 sc)

Round 4: [Sc in next 2 sts, inc] 6 times. (24 sc)

Rounds 5-14: *(10 rounds)* Sc in each st around. (24 sc)

Round 15: [Sc in next 2 sts, inv-dec] 6 times. (18 sc)

Start stuffing Body, adding more as you go.

Round 16: [Sc in next st, inv-dec] 6 times. (12 sc)

Round 17: [Inv-dec] 6 times. (6 sc)

Fasten off and close the opening securely. Leave a long end for sewing.

LEGS (Make 4)

Round 1: With MC, make a Magic Ring, 7 sc in ring. (7 sc)

Round 2: Working in back loops only, sc in each st around. (7 sc)

Rounds 3-4: *(2 rounds)* Sc in each st around. (7 sc)

Fasten off and leave a long end for sewing.

TAIL

Round 1: With Color A, make a Magic Ring, 8 sc in ring. (8 sc)

Rounds 2-3: *(2 rounds)* Sc in each st around. (8 sc)

Round 4: [Inv-dec] 2 times, sc in next 4 sts. (6 sc)

Fasten off and leave a long end for sewing.

DESIGNING THE FACE

Sewing on the Hair

Sew Hair onto the top of the Head. *(Image 7)*

Sewing on the Muzzle

Sew Muzzle between Rounds 11-13 on the front of the Head. *(Image 8)*

Eyes

With Color B and a yarn needle, make 8 vertical straight stitches (one-stitch in height) for each Eye on Round 10 (or one Round above the Muzzle). There should be 5 sts in between each eye. *(Image 9)*

Nose and Lips

With Color A and a yarn needle, make a straight stitch (2-stitches in height) in the shape of a "V" for the Nose, going from Round 10 and continuing onto the Muzzle on Round 11. It should be centered between the Eyes. *(Image 10)*

For the lips, make one long vertical straight stitch all the way to the bottom of the Muzzle, starting from the bottom point of the "V" stitch you made earlier for the Nose.

Adding Eye Whites

With Color A and a yarn needle, make one vertical straight stitch to the left of each Eye. *(Image 11)*

Sewing on the Ears

Sew the Ears onto the sides of the Head, one Round below where the Hair ends. *(Image 12)*

Sewing on the Cheeks

Sew Cheeks onto Head, beside each end of the Muzzle. *(Image 13)*

FINAL ASSEMBLY

1. Sew Body onto the Head. Make sure to position the Head to the right side of the Body, with the Body facing sideways, and the Head turned towards you. *(Image 14)*

2. Sew Legs onto the bottom of the Body. *(Image 15)*

3. Sew tail onto the back end of the Body. *(Image 16)*

11CM HEIGHT

Skill Level

Easy

BILLIE THE BEE

Billie is a busy bee who enjoys buzzing around in search of big and beautiful flowers.

Finished Size: About 2.6" (7.5 cm) tall

MATERIALS & TOOLS

HELLO COTTON YARN

- **Main colour (MC):** Yellow (123) - Body
- **Colour A:** Dark Brown (126) - for Stripes
- **Colour B:** White (154) - for Eye Whites and Wings
- **Colour C:** Orange-Red (115) - for Blush

HOOK SIZE
2.5 mm hook

OTHER
Toy Stuffing
Tapestry Needle
Stitch Marker

BODY

Round 1: With MC, make a magic ring, 6 sc in ring. (6 sc)

Round 2: Inc in each st around. (12 sc)

Round 3: [Sc in next st, inc] 6 times. (18 sc)

Round 4: [Sc in next 2 sts, inc] 6 times. (24 sc)

Round 5: [Sc in next 3 sts, inc] 6 times. (30 sc)

Round 6: [Sc in next 4 sts, inc] 6 times. (36 sc)

Rounds 7-11: *(5 rounds)* Sc in each st around. (36 sc)

Rounds 12-13: *(2 rounds)* Change to Color A. Sc in each st around. (36 sc) *(Image 1)*

Rounds 14-15: *(2 rounds)* Change to MC. Sc in each st around. (36 sc)

Rounds 16-17: *(2 rounds)* Change to Color A. Sc in each st around. (36 sc) *(Image 2)*

Rounds 18-19: *(2 rounds)* Change to MC. Sc in each st around. (36 sc)

Rounds 20-21: *(2 rounds)* Change to Color A. Sc in each st around. (36 sc) *(Image 3)*

Round 22: Change to MC. [Sc in next 4 sts, inv-dec] 6 times. (30 sc) *(Image 4)*

57

Round 23: [Sc in next 3 sts, inv-dec] 6 times. (24 sc)

Round 24: [Sc in next 2 sts, inv-dec] 6 times. (18 sc) Start stuffing Body, adding more as you go. *(Image 5)*

Round 25: [Sc in next st, inv-dec] 6 times. (12 sc)

Round 26: [Inv-dec] 6 times. (6 sc)

Fasten off and close the opening securely. *(Image 6)*

Gently use your hands to squeeze and re-shape the Body to flatten and widen the part that will be facing you. *(Image 7)*

DESIGNING THE FACE

Eyes

1. With Color A and a tapestry needle, make 4 vertical Straight Stitches (one-stitch in height) for each Eye, centered at the bottom of Round 5 and Round 9. There should be a spacing of about 3-4 rows in between each Eye. *(Image 8)*

2. With Color B, make 1 vertical Straight Stitch to the side of each Eye for the eye whites. *(Image 9)*

Lips

1. To sew the Lips, you will need to split Color A up to thinner strands. *(Image 10)*

2. Take 3 of the strands and make a horizontal Back Stitch (2-stitches-long) across Rounds 7 and 8, centered between the Eyes. *(Image 11)*

Blush

1. With Color C, sew on a horizontal Back Stitch (go over 2 times) near the sides of each Eye. *(Image 12)*

WINGS (Make 2)

Round 1: With Color B, make a magic ring, 8 sc in ring. (8 sc)

Fasten off and leave a tail for sewing.

FINAL ASSEMBLY

1. Sew Wings, side-by-side, onto the top of the Body, near Rounds 12-16. *(Images 13-14)*

2. And you're all done! *(Image 15)*

7CM HEIGHT

Skill Level

Intermediate

LUCY THE LLAMA

Lucy doesn't like to exercise. But when she needs to run, she can run faster than the fastest human on Earth!

Finished Size: About 5.5" (14.5 cm) tall

MATERIALS & TOOLS

HELLO COTTON YARN

Main colour (MC): Off-white (155) - Head, Body and Saddle

Colour A: Sand Beige (157) - Ears, Muzzle, Legs and Tail

Colour B: Dark Brown (126) - Eyes, Nose and Lips

Colour C: Turquoise (134) - Flower and Saddle Detailing

HOOK SIZE
2.5 mm hook

OTHER
Toy Stuffing

Tapestry Needle

Stitch Marker

HEAD

Round 1: With MC, make a magic ring, 6 sc in ring. (6 sc)

Round 2: Inc in each st around. (12 sc)

Round 3: [Sc in next st, inc] 6 times. (18 sc)

Round 4: [Sc in next 2 sts, inc] 6 times. (24 sc)

Round 5: [Sc in next 3 sts, inc] 6 times. (30 sc)

Rounds 6-9: *(4 rounds)* Sc in each st around. (30 sc)

Round 10: Sc in next 9 sts, inc in next 3 sts, sc in next 6 sts, inc in next 3 sts, sc in next 9 sts. (36 sc)

Round 11: [Sc in next 10 sts, inc in next 3 sts] 2 times, sc in next 10 sts. (42 sc)

Rounds 12-14: *(3 rounds)* Sc in each st around. (42 sc) *(Image 1)*

Round 15: Sc in next 10 sts, [inv-dec] 3 times, sc in next 10 sts, [inv-dec] 3 times, sc in next 10 sts. (36 sc)

Round 16: Sc in next 9 sts, [inv-dec] 3 times, sc in next 6 sts, [inv-dec] 3 times, sc in next 9 sts. (30 sc)

Round 17: [Sc in next 3 sts, inv-dec] 6 times. (24 sc)

Round 18: [Sc in next 2 sts, inv-dec] 6 times. (18 sc)

Start stuffing Head, adding more as you go. *(Image 2)*

At this point, gently use your hands to squeeze and re-shape the Head to give it an oval-like appearance (when viewed from the top). *(Image 3)*

Round 19: [Sc in next st, inv-dec] 6 times. (12 sc)

Round 20: [Inv-dec] 6 times. (6 sc)

Fasten off and close the opening securely.

MUZZLE

Round 1: With Color A, make a magic ring, 6 sc in ring. (6 sc)

Round 2: Inc in each st around. (12 sc)

Round 3: [Sc in next st, inc] 6 times. (18 sc) Clean fasten off and leave a long tail for sewing.

61

ADDING NOSE + LIPS ONTO THE MUZZLE

1. With Color B, make a "Y" shape with backstitches at the center of the Muzzle. *(Image 4)*

2. Knot ends at the back and trim excess.

EARS (Make 2)

Round 1: With Color A, make a magic ring, 3 sc in ring. (3 sc)

Round 2: Inc in each st around. (6 sc)

Rounds 3-5: *(3 rounds)* Sc in each st around. (6 sc)

Fasten off, leaving a tail for sewing. No stuffing required.

FLOWER

Round 1: With Color C, make a magic ring, [ch 5, sl st to the ring] 5 times to.

Pull magic ring to close. Fasten off, leaving a tail for sewing. *(Images 5-6)*

DESIGNING THE FACE

Sewing on the Muzzle

Sew Muzzle between Rounds 10-14 on the front of the Head. *(Image 7)*

Eyes

With Color B and a tapestry needle, make 4 diagonal stitches (one-stitch in height) for each Eye on Round 11, about one-stitch away from each side of the Muzzle. *(Image 8)*

Sewing on the Ears

Sew the Ears onto the top of the Head, near Rounds 2-3. *(Image 9)*

Sewing on the Flower

Sew Flower near the bottom of the left Ear. *(Image 10)*

BODY

Round 1: With MC, ch 13, sl st to form a ring. Ch 1, sc in each st around, sl st to first st. (12 sc) *(Image 11)*

Rounds 2-4: *(3 rounds)* Ch 1, sc in each st around, sl st to first st. (12 sc) *(Image 12)*

Round 5: Ch 8, starting in 2nd ch from hook, sc in next 7 ch, sl st in same st as starting ch, sc in the next 12 sts around the neck. (19 sc) *(Image 13)*

Round 6: Move stitch marker to the first st in this round. Sc in the next 6 sts, 3 sc in the next st, sc in the next 20 sts. (29 sc)

Rounds 7-9: *(3 rounds)* Sc in each st around. (29 sc) *(Image 14)*

Round 10: Sc in next 6 sts, [inv-dec] 3 times, sc in next 9 sts, [inv-dec] 2 times, sc in next 4 sts. (24 sc)

Round 11: [Sc in next 2 sts, inv-dec] 6 times. (18 sc) Start stuffing Body, adding more as you go.

Round 12: [Sc in next st, inv-dec] 6 times. (12 sc)

Round 13: [Inv-dec] 6 times. (6 sc)

Fasten off and close the opening securely. You can add more stuffing through the open neck.

LEGS (Make 4)

Round 1: With Color A, make a magic ring, 7 sc in ring. (7 sc)

Rounds 2-4: *(3 rounds)* Sc in each st around. (7 sc)

Fasten off, leaving a tail for sewing. Don't stuff Legs.

SADDLE

Round 1: With MC, ch 10; starting in 2nd ch from hook, sc in next 8 ch, 3 sc in last ch, working on other side of starting chain, sc in next 7 ch, inc in last ch. (20 sc)

Round 2: Inc in first st, sc in next 8 sts, inc in next 2 sts, sc in next 8 sts, inc in final st. (24 sc) Clean fasten off and leave a long tail for sewing.

13CM HEIGHT

ADDING DETAILS TO THE SADDLE

With Color C and tapestry needle, embroider small Back Stitches all around the Saddle at the bottom of Round 1. *(Image 15)*

TAIL

Round 1: With Color A, ch 4, starting in 2nd ch from hook, hdc in each ch across. (3 hdc) Fasten off. Fold the Tail in half and Whip Stitch the ends together.

Leave a tail for sewing.

FINAL ASSEMBLY

1. Sew Body onto the Head. Make sure the Body is facing sideways, and the Head is turned towards you. *(Image 16)*
2. Sew Legs to the Bottom of the Body. *(Image 17)*
3. Sew Tail to the back of the Body. *(Image 18)*
4. Sew Saddle onto the Body. *(Image 19)*
5. **Optional:** With a cotton bud tip and make-up blusher, add a pop of pink onto the cheeks for extra cuteness.
6. All done! *(Image 20)*

Skill Level

Intermediate

MOTHER HEN & BABY CHICK

Baby likes to follow Mommy wherever she goes.
Mommy loves the attention, of course!

Finished Size: About 5.5" (14.5 cm) tall

MATERIALS & TOOLS

HELLO COTTON YARN

Main colour (MC): White (154) – Body for Mother Hen and Wings

Colour A: Yellow (123) – Body for Baby Chick and Frill

Colour B: Orange-Red (115) – Beak and Frill

Colour C: Dark Brown (126) – Eyelids and Feet

HOOK SIZE
2.5 mm hook

OTHER
Toy Stuffing
Tapestry Needle
Stitch Marker

MOTHER HEN

BODY

Round 1: With MC, make a magic ring, 6 sc in ring. (6 sc)

Round 2: Inc in each st around. (12 sc)

Round 3: [Sc in next st, inc] 6 times. (18 sc)

Round 4: [Sc in next 2 sts, inc] 6 times. (24 sc)

Round 5: [Sc in next 3 sts, inc] 6 times. (30 sc)

Round 6: [Sc in next 4 sts, inc] 6 times. (36 sc)

Round 7: [Sc in next 5 sts, inc] 6 times. (42 sc)

Round 8: [Sc in next 6 sts, inc] 6 times. (48 sc)

Rounds 9-17: *(9 rounds)* Sc in each st around. (48 sc) *(Image 1)*

Round 18: [Sc in next 6 sts, inv-dec] 6 times. (42 sc)

Round 19: [Sc in next 5 sts, inv-dec] 6 times. (36 sc)

Round 20: [Sc in next 4 sts, inv-dec] 6 times. (30 sc)

Round 21: [Sc in next 3 sts, inv-dec] 6 times. (24 sc)

Round 22: [Sc in next 2 sts, inv-dec] 6 times. (18 sc)

Start stuffing Body, adding more as you go. *(Image 2)*

At this point, gently use your hands to squeeze and re-shape the Body to give it an oval-like appearance (when viewed from the top). *(Image 3)*

Round 23: [Sc in next st, inv-dec] 6 times. (12 sc)

Round 24: [Inv-dec] 6 times. (6 sc)

Fasten off and close the opening securely. *(Image 4)*

BEAK

Round 1: With Color B make a magic ring, 7 sc in ring. (7 sc)
Clean fasten off and leave a tail for sewing.

65

DESIGNING THE FACE

Sewing on the beak

Position Beak at the center of the Body, on Rounds 13-14 and sew in place. *(Image 5)*

Closed Eyelids

1. To sew the Eyelids, you will need to split Color C up to thinner strands. *(Image 6)*

2. Take 5 of the strands and make a diagonal Back Stitch (2-stitches-long) across Round 14. *(Image 7)*

3. Go back up to cinch the center of the Eyelid with a small Back Stitch. This will turn the Eyelid into an "L" shape. *(Image 8)*

4. Knot ends and hide inside the Body.

FEET

With a full strand of Color C, sew on the Feet near Rounds 19-21, using Back Stitches (2-stitches-tall) to form a downwards-pointing arrow shape. Use the position of the Eyelids as guidance on where to position the Feet. *(Image 9)*

FRILL

Round 1: With Color B, ch 10; starting in 2nd ch from hook, hdc in next 3 ch, skip next st, sl st in next st (first frill is made), [ch 4, starting in second ch from hook, hdc in each ch across (3 hdc), skip next st, sl st in next st] two times (to make the second and third frill. *(Image 10)*

Fasten off and leave a long tail for sewing.

SEWING ON THE FRILL

- Position the Frill at the top of the Body and sew in place. *(Images 11 & 12)*

WINGS (Make 2)

Round 1: With MC, make a magic ring, 5 sc in ring. (5 sc)

Round 2: Inc in each st around. (10 sc)

Rounds 3-4: *(2 rounds)* Sc in each st around. (10 sc) Fasten off and leave a long tail for sewing.

Flatten piece.

FINAL ASSEMBLY

1. Sew Wings to the sides of the Body, below Round 14, about 2 stitches away from each Eyelid. *(Image 13)*

2. Optional: With a cotton bud tip and make-up blusher, add a pop of pink onto the cheeks for extra cuteness. *(Image 14)*

3. All done! *(Image 15)*

BABY CHICK

BODY

Round 1: With Color A, make a magic ring, 6 sc in ring. (6 sc)

Round 2: Inc in each st around. (12 sc)

Round 3: [Sc in next st, inc] 6 times. (18 sc)

Round 4: [Sc in next 2 sts, inc] 6 times. (24 sc)

Round 5: [Sc in next 3 sts, inc] 6 times. (30 sc)

Rounds 6-11: *(6 rounds)* Sc in each st around. (30 sc)

Round 12: [Sc in next 3 sts, inv-dec] 6 times. (24 sc)

Round 13: [Sc in next 2 sts, inv-dec] 6 times. (18 sc) Start stuffing Body, adding more as you go.

Round 14: [Sc in next st, inv-dec] 6 times. (12 sc)

Round 15: [Inv-dec] 6 times. (6 sc)

Fasten off and close the opening securely.

BEAK

Round 1: With Color B make a magic ring, 5 sc in ring. (5 sc) Clean fasten off and leave a tail for sewing.

FRILL

Round 1: With Color A, [ch 4; starting in 2nd ch from hook, sl st in each ch across (3 sl st)] two times.

Fasten off and leave a tail for sewing.

DESIGNING THE FACE

Sewing on the beak

Position Beak at the center of the Body, on Rounds 8-9 and sew in place.

Closed Eyelids

1. To sew the Eyelids, you will need to split Color C up to thinnerstrands.

2. Take 5 of the strands and make a diagonal Back Stitch (2-stitches-long) across Round 9. *(Image 16)*

3. Knot ends and hide inside the Body.

SEWING ON THE FRILL

Position the Frill at the top of the Body and sew in place. *(Image 17)*

BLUSH

Optional: With a cotton bud tip and make-up blusher, add a pop of pink onto the cheeks for extra cuteness. *(Image 18)*

FEET

With a full strand of Color C, sew on the Feet on Round 12, using Back Stitches (1-stitch-tall) to form a downwards-pointing arrow shape. Use the position of the Eyelids as guidance on where to position the Feet. And you're all done! *(Images 19 & 20)*

Skill Level
★★☆
Intermediate

CHARLIE THE CAT

Charlie loves playing catch and can never resist a ball of yarn.

Finished Size: About 5.5" (14.5 cm) tall

MATERIALS & TOOLS

HELLO COTTON YARN

Main colour (MC): Off-White (155) - Head, Body, Arms, and Feet

Colour A: Ash Brown (128) - Patch, Arms, Ear and Tail

Colour B: Light Pink (101) - Blush

Colour C: Black (160) - Eyes and Ear

HOOK SIZE
2.5 mm hook

OTHER
Toy Stuffing
Tapestry Needle
Stitch Marker

HEAD

Round 1: With MC, make a magic ring, 6 sc in ring. (6 sc)

Round 2: Inc in each st around. (12 sc)

Round 3: [Sc in next st, inc] 6 times. (18 sc)

Round 4: [Sc in next 2 sts, inc] 2 times, change to Color A, [sc in next 2 sts, inc], change back to MC, [sc in next 2 sts, inc] 3 times. (24 sc)

Round 5: [Sc in next 3 sts, inc] 2 times, change to Color A, [sc in next 3 sts, inc], change back to MC, [sc in next 3 sts, inc] 3 times. (30 sc)

Round 6: [Sc in next 4 sts, inc] 2 times, change to Color A, [sc in next 4 sts, inc], change back to MC, [sc in next 4 sts, inc] 3 times. (36 sc)

Round 7: [Sc in next 5 sts, inc] 2 times, change to Color A, [sc in next 5 sts, inc], change back to MC, [sc in next 5 sts, inc] 3 times. (42 sc)

Round 8: Sc in next 14 sts, change to Color A, sc in next 7 sts, change back to MC, sc in next 21 sts. (42 sc) *(Image 1)*

You can now knot and trim off Color A as you won't be using it anymore for the Head.

Rounds 9-14: *(6 rounds)* Sc in each st around. (42 sc) *(Image 2)*

Round 15: [Sc in next 5 sts, inv-dec] 6 times. (36 sc)

Round 16: [Sc in next 4 sts, inv-dec] 6 times. (30 sc)

Round 17: [Sc in next 3 sts, inv-dec] 6 times. (24 sc)

Round 18: [Sc in next 2 sts, inv-dec] 6 times. (18 sc)
Start stuffing Head, adding more as you go.

At this point, gently use your hands to squeeze and re-shape the Head to give it an oval-like appearance (when viewed from the top). *(Images 3 & 4)*

Round 19: [Sc in next st, inv-dec] 6 times. (12 sc)

Round 20: [Inv-dec] 6 times. (6 sc)

Fasten off and close the opening securely.

69

MUZZLE

Round 1: With MC, make a magic ring, 5 sc in ring. (5 sc)

Round 2: Inc in each st around. (10 sc)

Clean fasten off and leave a tail for sewing.

BLUSH (Make 2)

Round 1: With Color B, make a magic ring, 5 sc in ring. (5 sc) Fasten off and leave a tail for sewing.

EARS (Make 2, one in Color A and one in Color C)

Round 1: With Color A/C, make a magic ring, 3 sc in ring. (3 sc)

Round 2: Inc in each st around. (6 sc)

Round 3: [Sc in next st, inc] 3 times. (9 sc)

Round 4: Sc in each st around. (9 sc)

Fasten off and leave a tail for sewing.

Don't stuff Ears. Flatten the piece.

DESIGNING THE FACE

Sewing on the Nose and Lips

1. With Color B and your darning needle, embroider a "V" shape for the Nose onto the Muzzle, using Back Stitches (3 Back Stitches for each side of the "V"). *(Image 5)*

2. To sew the Lips, you will need to split Color C up to thinner strands. *(Image 6)*

3. Take 4 of the strands and embroider a "U" shape for the Lips onto the Muzzle, using backstitches. *(Image 7)*

4. Knot all ends at the back and trim excess.

Sewing on the Muzzle

Position Muzzle near Round 13 at the center of the Head and sew it on. *(Image 8)*

Eyes

With a full strand of Color C, make 5 vertical Straight Stitches (one-stitch in height) for each Eye on Round 13, approximately two-stitches away from each end of the Muzzle. *(Image 9)*

Knot ends at the bottom of the Head and trim excess.

Sewing on the Blush

Sew on Blush pieces below each Eye. *(Image 10)*

Sewing on the Whiskers

- To sew the Whiskers, you will need to split Color C up to thinnerstrands.

- Take 4 of the strands and make a horizontal Back Stitch (3-stitches-long) at the bottom of Rounds 13 and 14, on each side of the Head (about three stitches away from the Eyes). *(Image 11)*

- Knot ends at the bottom of Head and trim excess.

Sewing on the Ears

Sew on Ears to the top of the Head, near Rounds 4-8 (on each side of the Head). *(Image 12)*

BODY

Round 1: With MC, make a magic ring, 6 sc in ring. (6 sc)

Round 2: Inc in each st around. (12 sc)

Round 3: [Sc in next st, inc] 6 times. (18 sc)

Round 4: [Sc in next 2 sts, inc] 6 times. (24 sc)

Rounds 5-8: *(4 rounds)* Sc in each st around. (24 sc) Change to Color A.

Round 9: Sc in each st around. (24 sc)

Round 10: [Sc in next 2 sts, inv-dec] 6 times. (18 sc) Fasten off and leave a long tail for sewing. Stuff Body firmly.

ARMS (Make 2, one in MC and one in Color A)

Round 1: With MC/Color A, make a magic ring, 7 sc in ring. (7 sc)

Rounds 2-5: *(4 rounds)* Sc in each st around. (7 sc)

Fasten off and leave a tail for sewing. Don't stuff Arms.

FEET (Make 2)

Round 1: With MC, make a magic ring, 5 sc in ring. (5 sc)

Round 2: Inc in each st around. (10 sc)

Round 3: Sc in each st around. (10 sc)

Round 4: [Inv-dec] 5 times. (5 sc) Don't stuff Feet

Fasten off and close the opening securely. Flatten piece. Leave a tail for sewing.

TAIL

Row 1: With Color A, ch 20; starting in 2nd ch from hook, hdc in each ch across. (19 hdc)

Fasten off and leave a tail for sewing. The piece should curl naturally on its own.

FINAL ASSEMBLY

1. Sew Body onto the Head. *(Image 13)*

2. Sew Arms onto the Body. *(Image 14)*

3. Sew Feet onto the lower part of the Body. *(Image 15)*

4. Sew Tail to the back of the Body. *(Image 16)*

5. All done!

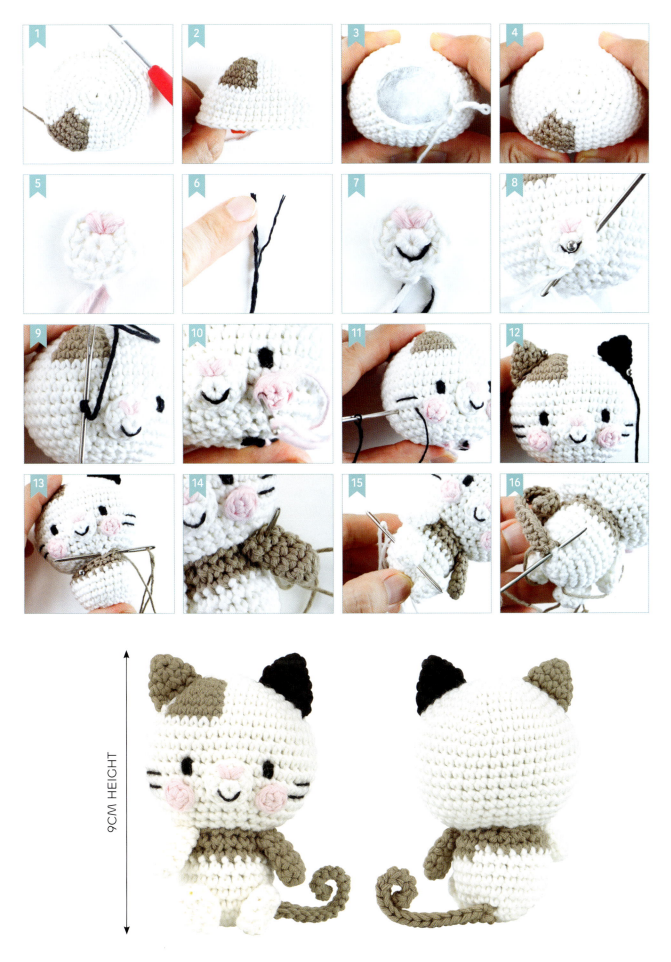

Skill Level
★★☆
Intermediate

KELLY THE KOALA

Kelly has a special talent: falling asleep anytime, anywhere, even when she's halfway munching on a leaf.

Finished Size: About 3.6" (9.5 cm) tall

MATERIALS & TOOLS

HELLO COTTON YARN

- **Main colour (MC):** Grey (159) - Head, Body, Arms, Feet, Ears and Tail
- **Colour A:** Black (160) - Nose and Eyes
- **Colour B:** Light Pink (101) - Blush Color
- **Colour C:** Forest Green (137) - Leaves

HOOK SIZE
2.5 mm hook

OTHER
Toy Stuffing
Tapestry Needle
Stitch Marker

HEAD

Round 1: With MC, make a magic ring, 6 sc in ring. (6 sc)
Round 2: Inc in each st around. (12 sc)
Round 3: [Sc in next st, inc] 6 times. (18 sc)
Round 4: [Sc in next 2 sts, inc] 6 times. (24 sc)
Round 5: [Sc in next 3 sts, inc] 6 times. (30 sc)
Round 6: [Sc in next 4 sts, inc] 6 times. (36 sc)
Round 7: [Sc in next 5 sts, inc] 6 times. (42 sc)
Rounds 8-14: *(7 rounds)* Sc in each st around. (42 sc)
Round 15: [Sc in next 5 sts, inv-dec] 6 times. (36 sc)
Round 16: [Sc in next 4 sts, inv-dec] 6 times. (30 sc)
Round 17: [Sc in next 3 sts, inv-dec] 6 times. (24 sc)
Round 18: [Sc in next 2 sts, inv-dec] 6 times. (18 sc) *(Image 1)* Start stuffing Head, adding more as you go. *(Image 2)*

At this point, gently use your hands to squeeze and re-shape the Head to give it an oval-like appearance (when viewed from the top). *(Images 3 & 4)*

Round 19: [Sc in next st, inv-dec] 6 times. (12 sc)
Round 20: [Inv-dec] 6 times. (6 sc)
Fasten off and close the opening securely.

NOSE

Round 1: With Color A, ch 7; starting in 2nd ch from hook, sc in next 5 ch, 3 sc in last ch, working on other side of starting chain, sc in next 4 ch, inc in last ch. (14 sc)
Round 2: Inc in first st, sc in next 5 sts, inc in next 2 sts, sc in the next 6 sts. (17 sc)
Clean fasten off and leave a tail for sewing.

BLUSH (Make 2)

Round 1: With Color B, make a magic ring, 5 sc in ring. (5 sc)
Fasten off and leave a tail for sewing.

73

EARS (Make 2)

Round 1: With MC, make a magic ring, 6 sc in ring. (6 sc)
Round 2: Inc in each st around. (12 sc)
Round 3: [Sc in next st, inc] 6 times. (18 sc)
Round 4: [Sc in next 2 sts, inc] 6 times. (24 sc)
Rounds 5-7: *(3 rounds)* Sc in each st around. (24 sc)
Don't stuff Ears.
Flatten the piece and give it a squeeze to curve the Ear inwards. *(Image 5)*

DESIGNING THE FACE

Sewing on the Nose

Position the Nose on Rounds 9-15. The short side of the Nose should be pointing downwards. Sew in place. *(Image 6)*

Eyelids

1. To sew the Eyelids, you will need to split Color A up to thinner strands. *(Image 7)*
2. Take 6 of the strands and make a diagonal Back Stitch (3-stitches-long) across Round 13 for each Eyelid, to the sides of each end of the Nose. *(Image 8)*
3. Knot ends and hide inside Head.

Sewing on the Blush

Sew on Blush pieces below each Eye. *(Image 9)*

Sewing on the Ears

Sew on Ears to the sides of the Head, between Rounds 10-16, about 5-6 stitches away from each Eyelid. *(Image 10)*

BODY

Round 1: With MC, make a magic ring, 6 sc in ring. (6 sc)
Round 2: Inc in each st around. (12 sc)
Round 3: [Sc in next st, inc] 6 times. (18 sc)
Round 4: [Sc in next 2 sts, inc] 6 times. (24 sc)
Rounds 5-9: *(5 rounds)* Sc in each st around. (24 sc)
Round 10: [Sc in next 2 sts, inv-dec] 6 times. (18 sc)
Fasten off and leave a long tail for sewing.
Stuff Body firmly.

ARMS (Make 2)

Round 1: With MC, make a magic ring, 7 sc in ring. (7 sc)
Rounds 2-5: *(4 rounds)* Sc in each st around. (7 sc)
Fasten off and leave a tail for sewing.
Don't stuff Arms.

FEET (Make 2)

Round 1: With MC, make a magic ring, 5 sc in ring. (5 sc)
Round 2: Inc in each st around. (10 sc)
Round 3: Sc in each st around. (10 sc)
Round 4: [Inv-dec] 5 times. (5 sc) Don't stuff Feet
Fasten off and close the opening securely. Flatten piece. Leave a tail for sewing.

LEAVES

First leaf: With Color C, ch 5; starting in 2nd ch from hook, sl st in first ch, hdc in next ch, dc in next ch then sl st in the same ch. Continue on with the second leaf.

Second leaf: Ch 5; starting in 2nd ch from hook, sl st in first ch, hdc in next ch, dc in next ch then sl st in the same ch. Sl st to the bottom of the first leaf. Continue on to make the stem.

Stem: Ch 8; starting in 2nd ch from hook, sl st in each ch across. Then make one more sl st to the bottom of the first leaf.
Fasten off and leave a long tail for sewing.

Tail

Round 1: With MC, make a magic ring, 7 sc in ring. (7 sc).
Round 2: Sc in each st around. (7 sc)
Fasten off and leave a tail for sewing.

FINAL ASSEMBLY

1. Sew Body onto the Head. *(Image 11)*
2. Sew Arms onto the sides of the Body. *(Image 12)*
3. Sew Leaves, between the Arms. *(Image 13)*
4. Sew Feet onto the lower part of the Body, to the sides. *(Image 14)*
5. Sew Tail to the side of the Body. *(Image 15)*
6. All done! *(Image 16)*

8CM HEIGHT

Skill Level

Intermediate

PEPPER THE PUPPY

Pepper loves walks in the sunset and ending his day
with a banana oatmeal snack.

Finished Size: About 4.3" (11.5 cm) tall

MATERIALS & TOOLS

HELLO COTTON YARN

Main colour (MC): Light Brown (165) - Head, Body, Legs, Ears and Tail

Colour A: Off-white (155) - Head, Muzzle and Body

Colour B: Peach Pink (112) - Blush

Colour C: Black (160) - Eyes and Nose

HOOK SIZE
2.5 mm hook

OTHER
Toy Stuffing
Tapestry Needle
Stitch Marker

HEAD

Round 1: With MC, make a magic ring, 6 sc in ring. (6 sc)
Round 2: Inc in each st around. (12 sc)
Round 3: [Sc in next st, inc] 6 times. (18 sc)
Round 4: [Sc in next 2 sts, inc] 6 times. (24 sc)
Round 5: [Sc in next 3 sts, inc] 6 times. (30 sc)
Round 6: [Sc in next 4 sts, inc] 6 times. (36 sc)
Round 7: [Sc in next 5 sts, inc] 6 times. (42 sc)
Rounds 8-13: *(6 rounds)* Sc in each st around. (42 sc)
Round 14: Change to color A. Sc in each st around. (42 sc) *(Image 1)*
Round 15: [Sc in next 5 sts, inv-dec] 6 times. (36 sc)
Round 16: [Sc in next 4 sts, inv-dec] 6 times. (30 sc)
Round 17: [Sc in next 3 sts, inv-dec] 6 times. (24 sc)
Round 18: [Sc in next 2 sts, inv-dec] 6 times. (18 sc)
Start stuffing Head, adding more as you go. *(Image 2)*
Round 19: [Sc in next st, inv-dec] 6 times. (12 sc)
Round 20: [Inv-dec] 6 times. (6 sc)
Fasten off and close the opening securely.

MUZZLE

Round 1: With Color A, make a magic ring, 5 sc in ring. (5 sc)
Round 2: Inc in each st around. (10 sc)
Rounds 3-4: *(2 rounds)* Sc in each st around. (10 sc)
Fasten off, leaving a long tail for sewing.
Stuff lightly.

NOSE

Round 1: With Color C, make a magic ring, 5 sc in ring. (5 sc)
Fasten off, leaving a tail for sewing.

BLUSH (Make 2)

Round 1: With Color B, make a magic ring, 5 sc in ring. (5 sc) Fasten off, leaving a tail for sewing.

77

EARS (Make 2)

Round 1: With MC, make a magic ring, 3 sc in ring. (3 sc)

Round 2: Inc in each st around. (6 sc)

Round 3: [Sc in next st, inc] 3 times. (9 sc)

Round 4: [Sc in next 2 sts, inc] 3 times. (12 sc) Fasten off, leaving a long tail for sewing.

Don't stuff Ears. Flatten piece.

DESIGNING THE FACE

Assembling Nose + Muzzle

Sew Nose onto one side of the Muzzle *(Image 3)*

Sewing Muzzle onto Head

Position Muzzle at the center of the Head, near Rounds 14-16 and sew in place. *(Images 4 & 5)*

Eyes

With Color C, make 4 diagonal stitches (one-stitch in height) for each Eye on Round 14, approximately two-stitches away from each side of the Muzzle. *(Image 6)*

Sewing on the Blush

Sew on Blush pieces below each Eye. *(Image 7)*

Sewing on the Ears

Sew on Ears at the top of the Head, near Rounds 4-7 (on each side of the Head). *(Image 8)*

BODY

Round 1: With MC, make a magic ring, 6 sc in ring. (6 sc)

Round 2: Inc in each st around. (12 sc)

Round 3: [Sc in next st, inc] 6 times. (18 sc)

Round 4: [Sc in next 2 sts, inc] 6 times. (24 sc)

Round 5: Sc in each st around. (24 sc)

Rounds 6-12: *(7 rounds)* Change to Color A. Sc in next 6 sts, change back to MC, sc in next 18 sts. (24 sc)

Round 13: [Sc in next 2 sts, inv-dec] 6 times. (18 sc) *(Image 9)*

Start stuffing Body, adding more as you go. *(Image 10)*

Round 14: [Sc in next st, inv-dec] 6 times. (12 sc)

Round 15: [Inv-dec] 6 times. (6 sc)

Fasten off and close the opening securely. *(Image 11)*

LEGS (Make 4)

Round 1: With MC, make a magic ring, 7 sc in ring. (7 sc)

Rounds 2-3: *(2 rounds)* Sc in each st around. (7 sc)

Fasten off, leaving a long tail for sewing.

Don't stuff Legs.

TAIL

Row 1: With MC, ch 12; starting in 2nd ch from hook, hdc in each ch across. (11 hdc)

Fasten off, leaving a tail for sewing.

The piece should curl naturally on its own.

FINAL ASSEMBLY

1. Sew Body onto the Head. Make sure to position the Head to the right side of the Body, with the Body facing sideways, and the Head turned towards you. *(Images 12 & 13)*

2. Sew Legs to the bottom of the Body. *(Image 14)*

3. Sew Tail to the back of the Body. *(Image 15)*

4. All done! *(Image 16)*

Skill Level

Intermediate

GRACIE THE GIRAFFE

This baby giraffe is still precious and small, but soon enough she'll be the tallest of them all.

Finished Size: About 5.3" (14.2 cm) tall

MATERIALS & TOOLS

HELLO COTTON YARN

- **Main colour (MC):** Yellow (120) - Head, Ears, Body, Legs and Tail
- **Colour A:** Dark Brown (168) - Antlers, Spots, Legs and Tail
- **Colour B:** Sand Beige (157) - Muzzle
- **Colour C:** Black (160) - Eyes

HOOK SIZE

2.5 mm hook

OTHER

Toy Stuffing

Tapestry Needle

Stitch Marker

HEAD

Round 1: With MC, make a magic ring, 6 sc in ring. (6 sc)

Round 2: Inc in each st around. (12 sc)

Round 3: [Sc in next st, inc] 6 times. (18 sc)

Round 4: [Sc in next 2 sts, inc] 6 times. (24 sc)

Round 5: [Sc in next 3 sts, inc] 6 times. (30 sc)

Rounds 6-9: *(4 rounds)* Sc in each st around. (30 sc)

Round 10: Sc in next 9 sts, inc in next 3 sts, sc in next 6 sts, inc in next 3 sts, sc in next 9 sts. (36 sc)

Round 11: [Sc in next 10 sts, inc in next 3 sts] 2 times, sc in next 10 sts. (42 sc)

Rounds 12-14: *(3 rounds)* Sc in each st around. (42 sc) *(Image 1)*

Round 15: Sc in next 10 sts, [inv-dec] 3 times, sc in next 10 sts, [inv-dec] 3 times, sc in next 10 sts. (36 sc)

Round 16: Sc in next 9 sts, [inv-dec] 3 times, sc in next 6 sts, [inv-dec] 3 times, sc in next 9 sts. (30 sc)

Round 17: [Sc in next 3 sts, inv-dec] 6 times. (24 sc)

Round 18: [Sc in next 2 sts, inv-dec] 6 times. (18 sc)

Start stuffing Head, adding more as you go. *(Image 2)*

At this point, gently use your hands to squeeze and re-shape the Head to give it an oval-like appearance (when viewed from the top). *(Image 3)*

Round 19: [Sc in next st, inv-dec] 6 times. (12 sc)

Round 20: [Inv-dec] 6 times. (6 sc)

Fasten off and close the opening securely.

MUZZLE

Round 1: With Color B, ch 10; starting in 2nd ch from hook, sc in next 8 ch, 3 sc in last ch, working on other side of starting chain, sc in next 7 ch, inc in last ch. (20 sc)

Round 2: Inc in first st, sc in next 8 sts, then leave the remaining sts unworked. (10 sc)

Clean fasten off and leave a tail for sewing.

81

EARS (Make 2)

Row 1: With MC, ch 5; starting in 2nd ch from hook, sl st in first ch, sc in next ch, hdc in next ch and dc in last ch. (1 sl st, 1 sc, 1 hdc & 1 dc)

Fasten off and leave a tail for sewing.

ANTLERS (Make 2)

Row 1: With Color A, ch 4, starting in 2nd ch from hook, 4 hdc in next ch, sl st in same ch, sl st in next 2 ch. (4 hdc, 3 sl st) Fasten off and leave a tail for sewing.

DESIGNING THE FACE

Sewing on the Muzzle

Sew Muzzle between Rounds 12-14 on the front of the Head. *(Image 4)*

Eyes

With Color C and a tapestry needle, make 4 vertical straight stitches (one-stitch in height) for each Eye on Round 10. There should be 6 sts in between each eye. *(Image 5)*

Nostrils

With Color A and a tapestry needle, make 1 diagonal Back Stitch (one-stitch in height) for each Nostril on the Muzzle. Position them at the center of the Muzzle, with approximately 7 stitches between each Nostril. *(Image 6)*

Sewing on the Antlers

Sew the Antlers onto the top of the Head. *(Image 7)*

Sewing on the Ears

Sew the Ears onto the sides of the Head, on Rounds 6-7. *(Image 8)*

BODY

Round 1: With MC, make a magic ring, 6 sc in ring. (6 sc)
Round 2: Inc in each st around. (12 sc)
Round 3: [Sc in next st, inc] 6 times. (18 sc)
Round 4: [Sc in next 2 sts, inc] 6 times. (24 sc)
Rounds 5-10: *(6 rounds)* Sc in each st around. (24 sc)
Round 11: [Inv-dec] 3 times, sc in the next 18 sts. (21 sc)
Round 12: [Inv-dec] 3 times, sc in the next 15 sts. (18 sc)
Round 13: [Inv-dec] 3 times, sc in the next 12 sts. (15 sc)
Round 14: Sc in each st around. (15 sc)
Stuff firmly. *(Image 9)*

SMALL PATCH

Round 1: With Color A, make a magic ring, 5 sc in ring. (5 sc) Clean fasten off, leaving a tail for sewing.

BIG PATCH

Round 1: With Color A, make a magic ring, 5 sc in ring. (5 sc)

Round 2: Inc in each st around. (10 sc)
Clean fasten off, leaving a tail for sewing.

FRONT LEGS (Make 2)

Round 1: With Color A, make a magic ring, 5 sc in ring. (5 sc)
Round 2: Inc in each st around. (10 sc)
Round 3: Sc in each st around. (10 sc)
Round 4: Change to MC, sc in each st around. (10 sc)
Round 5: [Inv-dec] 3 times, sc in next 4 sts. (7 sc)
Rounds 6-7: *(2 rounds)* Sc in each st around. (7 sc)
Fasten off, leaving a tail for sewing.
Stuff lightly.

HIND LEGS (Make 2)

Round 1: With Color A, make a magic ring, 5 sc in ring. (5 sc)
Round 2: Inc in each st around. (10 sc)
Round 3: Sc in each st around. (10 sc)
Round 4: Change to MC, sc in each st around. (10 sc)
Round 5: [Inv-dec] 3 times, sc in next 4 sts. (7 sc)
Rounds 6-8: *(3 rounds)* Sc in each st around. (7 sc)
Fasten off, leaving a tail for sewing. Stuff lightly.

TAIL

Round 1: With Color A, make a magic ring, [ch 3, sl st to the ring] 5 times to. Pull magic ring to close. The shape will look like a flower with 5 petals. *(Images 10 & 11)*
Sl st to the ch space of the first petal.

Change to MC. Ch 8. *(Image 12)*
Fasten off, leaving a tail for sewing.
Knot the yarn ends and trim excess.

FINAL ASSEMBLY

1. Sew Body onto the Head. Make sure the Body is facing sideways, and the Head is turned towards you. *(Image 13)*

2. Sew Patches onto the Body. Position the Small Patch near Rounds 9-10, and sew it on off-center on the Body. For the Big Patch, sew it on near Rounds 5-7 with a one-stitch gap away from the Small Patch. *(Image 14)*

3. Sew Front Legs to the right side of the Body, side by side, near Round 9. *(Image 15)*

4. Sew Legs to the bottom of the Body, one at the front and one at the back (imagine the Legs in a seated position).

5. Sew Tail to the bottom of the Body. *(Image 16)*

6. Optional: With a cotton bud tip and make-up blusher, add a pop of pink onto the cheeks for extra cuteness.

Skill Level
★★☆
Intermediate

BEATRICE THE BUNNY

Whenever she hears the loud "crunch" of carrots, Beatrice will show up!

Finished Size: About 4.3" (12 cm) tall

MATERIALS & TOOLS

HELLO COTTON YARN

- **Main colour (MC):** Pink (102) - Head, Body, Arms, Feet, Ears and Tail
- **Colour A:** Orange-Red (115) - Blush and Carrot
- **Colour B:** Turquoise (134) - Carrot Leaves
- **Colour C:** Black (160) - Eyes and Lips

HOOK SIZE
2.5 mm hook

OTHER
Toy Stuffing
Tapestry Needle
Stitch Marker

HEAD

Round 1: With MC, make a magic ring, 6 sc in ring. (6 sc)
Round 2: Inc in each st around. (12 sc)
Round 3: [Sc in next st, inc] 6 times. (18 sc)
Round 4: [Sc in next 2 sts, inc] 6 times. (24 sc)
Round 5: [Sc in next 3 sts, inc] 6 times. (30 sc)
Round 6: [Sc in next 4 sts, inc] 6 times. (36 sc)
Round 7: [Sc in next 5 sts, inc] 6 times. (42 sc)
Rounds 8-14: *(7 rounds)* Sc in each st around. (42 sc) *(Image 1)*
Round 15: [Sc in next 5 sts, inv-dec] 6 times. (36 sc)
Round 16: [Sc in next 4 sts, inv-dec] 6 times. (30 sc)
Round 17: [Sc in next 3 sts, inv-dec] 6 times. (24 sc)
Round 18: [Sc in next 2 sts, inv-dec] 6 times. (18 sc)
Start stuffing Head, adding more as you go. *(Image 2)*
At this point, gently use your hands to squeeze and re-shape the Head to give it an oval-like appearance (when viewed from the top). *(Images 3 & 4)*

Round 19: [Sc in next st, inv-dec] 6 times. (12 sc)
Round 20: [Inv-dec] 6 times. (6 sc)
Fasten off and close the opening securely. *(Image 5)*

BLUSH (Make 2)
Round 1: With Color A, make a magic ring, 5 sc in ring. (5 sc) Fasten off and leave a tail for sewing.

EARS (Make 2)
Round 1: With MC, make a magic ring, 6 sc in ring. (6 sc)
Round 2: Inc in each st around. (12 sc)
Rounds 3-7: *(5 rounds)* Sc in each st around. (12 sc)
Fasten off and leave a long tail for sewing. Don't stuff Ears. Flatten the piece and give it a squeeze to curve the Ear inwards.

DESIGNING THE FACE
Lips
1. To sew the Lips, you will need to split Color C up to thinner strands. *(Image 6)*
2. Take 5 of the strands and make a "w" shape with Back Stitches on Round 14, at the center of the Head. *(Images 7-9)*
3. Knot ends and hide inside Head.

Eyes
1. With a full strand of Color C, make 3 vertical straight stitches (one-stitch in height) for each Eye on Round 13, approximately two-stitches away from each end of the Lips. There should be 6 sts in between each Eye. *(Image 10)*

Sewing on the Blush
Sew on Blush pieces below each Eye. *(Image 11)*

Sewing on the Ears
Sew on Ears at the top of the Head, near Round 3, with a gap of about 2-stitches between the Ears. *(Image 12)*

BODY
Round 1: With MC, make a magic ring, 6 sc in ring. (6 sc)
Round 2: Inc in each st around. (12 sc)
Round 3: [Sc in next st, inc] 6 times. (18 sc)
Round 4: [Sc in next 2 sts, inc] 6 times. (24 sc)
Rounds 5-9: *(5 rounds)* Sc in each st around. (24 sc)
Round 10: [Sc in next 2 sts, inv-dec] 6 times. (18 sc)
Fasten off and leave a long tail for sewing.
Stuff Body firmly.

ARMS (Make 2)
Round 1: With MC, make a magic ring, 7 sc in ring. (7 sc)
Rounds 2-5: *(4 rounds)* Sc in each st around. (7 sc)
Fasten off and leave a tail for sewing.
Don't stuff Arms.

FEET (Make 2)
Round 1: With MC, make a magic ring, 5 sc in ring. (5 sc)
Round 2: Inc in each st around. (10 sc)
Round 3: Sc in each st around. (10 sc)
Round 4: [Inv-dec] 5 times. (5 sc) Don't stuff Feet
Fasten off and close the opening securely.
Flatten piece. Leave a tail for sewing.

CARROT
Round 1: With Color A, make a magic ring, 3 sc in ring. (3 sc)
Round 2: Inc in each st around. (6 sc)
Round 3: Sc in each st around. (6 sc)
Round 4: [Sc in next st, inc] 3 times. (9 sc)
Rounds 5-6: *(2 rounds)* Sc in each st around. (9 sc)
Stuff Carrot. *(Image 13)*
Round 7: [Sc in next st, inv-dec] 3 times. (6 sc)
Change to Color B. Do not trim off Color A.
Round 8: Sl st in the first st, ch 6, sl st to the bottom of the same st, sl st in the next st, ch 6, sl st to the bottom of the same st, sl st in the next 4 sts. (6 sl st) *(Image 14)*
Fasten off and weave in ends.
Hide Color B in Carrot and trim excess yarn. Leave a tail of Color A for sewing.

TAIL
Round: With MC, make a magic ring, [ch 3, sl st to the ring] 5 times. Pull magic ring to close and fasten off, leaving a tail for sewing. The shape will look like a flower with 5 petals.

FINAL ASSEMBLY
1. Sew Body onto the Head. *(Image 15)*
2. Sew Carrot onto the center of the Body. *(Image 16)*
3. Sew Arms onto the Body, with the Carrot in between. *(Image 17)*
4. Sew Feet onto the lower part of the Body. *(Image 18)*
5. Sew Tail to the back of the body. *(Image 19)*
6. Optional: With a cotton bud tip and make-up blusher, add a pop of pink onto the inner part of the Ears for extra cuteness. *(Image 20)*
7. All done!

10CM HEIGHT

87

Skill Level

Intermediate

FRANCIS THE FROG

Francis is a handsome little frog who likes to daydream the day away.

Finished Size: About 4" (10 cm) tall

MATERIALS & TOOLS

HELLO COTTON YARN

Main colour (MC): Pastel Green (138) - Head, Body, Arms, and Feet

Colour A: White (154) - Body

Colour B: Peach Pink (112) - Blush and Bow

Colour C: Black (160) - Eyes, Lips and Stripes

HOOK SIZE
2.5 mm hook

OTHER
Toy Stuffing

Tapestry Needle

Stitch Marker

HEAD

Round 1: With MC, make a magic ring, 6 sc in ring. (6 sc)

Round 2: Inc in each st around. (12 sc)

Round 3: [Sc in next st, inc] 6 times. (18 sc)

Round 4: Sc in each st around. (18 sc)

Round 5: [Sc in next 2 sts, inc] 6 times. (24 sc)

Round 6: Sc in each st around. (24 sc)

Round 5: [Sc in next 3 sts, inc] 6 times. (30 sc)

Rounds 6-14: (9 rounds) Sc in each st around. (30 sc) *(Image 1)*

Round 15: [Sc in next 3 sts, inv-dec] 6 times. (24 sc)

Round 16: Sc in each st around. (24 sc)

Round 17: [Sc in next 2 sts, inv-dec] 6 times. (18 sc)

Round 18: Sc in each st around. (18 sc)

Start stuffing Head, adding more as you go. *(Image 2)*

Round 19: [Sc in next st, inv-dec] 6 times. (12 sc)

Round 20: Sc in each st around. (12 sc)

Round 21: [Inv-dec] 6 times. (6 sc)

Fasten off and close the opening securely.

Gently use your hands to squeeze and re-shape the Head to give it an oval-like appearance (when viewed from the top). *(Image 3)*

EYES (Make 2)

Round 1: With MC, make a magic ring, 5 sc in ring. (5 sc)

Round 2: Inc in each st around. (10 sc)

Rounds 3-4: *(2 rounds)* Sc in each st around. (10 sc) Fasten off and leave a tail for sewing.

Stuff lightly.

BLUSH (Make 2)

Round 1: With Color B, make a magic ring, 5 sc in ring. (5 sc) Fasten off and leave a tail for sewing.

DESIGNING THE FACE

Sewing on the Eyes

Sew on Eyes at the top of the Head, with a gap of 2 stitches between each Eye. *(Image 4)*

Sewing on the Eyelids and Lips

1. To sew the Eyelids, you will need to split Color C up to thinner strands. *(Image 5)*

2. Take 5 of the strands and make a diagonal Back Stitch (2-stitches-long) near the bottom of each Eye. *(Image 6)*

3. For the Lips, make a vertical Back Stitch near Round 12 of the Head, about 2 rows below the Eyes in the center. *(Image 7)*

4. Knot ends and hide inside Head.

Sewing on the Blush

Sew on Blush pieces below each Eye. *(Image 8)*

BODY

Round 1: With MC, make a magic ring, 6 sc in ring. (6 sc)

Round 2: Inc in each st around. (12 sc)

Round 3: [Sc in next st, inc] 6 times. (18 sc)

Round 4: [Sc in next 2 sts, inc] 6 times. (24 sc)

Rounds 5-6: *(2 rounds)* Sc in each st around. (24 sc) Change to Color A.

Rounds 7-9: *(3 rounds)* Sc in each st around. (24 sc)

Round 10: [Sc in next 2 sts, inv-dec] 6 times. (18 sc)

Fasten off and leave a long tail for sewing.

Adding Stripes to the Shirt/Body

With Color C and tapestry needle, embroider small Back Stitches around the Body on Rounds 7-8. Stuff Body firmly. *(Images 9 & 10)*

BOWTIE

Row 1: With Color B, ch 7; starting in 2nd ch from hook, sc in each st across. (6 sc)

Row 2: Ch 1, turn, sc in each st across. (6 sc)

Fasten off, leaving a long tail for sewing.

Twist the ends of Bowtie to form the shape. Wrap the tail about 3 times around the center and secure. *(Images 11 & 12)*

ARMS (Make 2)

Round 1: With MC, make a magic ring, 7 sc in ring. (7 sc)

Rounds 2-5: *(4 rounds)* Sc in each st around. (7 sc)

Fasten off, leaving a long tail for sewing.

Don't stuff Arms.

LEGS (Make 2)

Round 1: With MC, make a magic ring, 5 sc in ring. (5 sc)

Round 2: Inc in each st around. (10 sc)

Round 3: Sc in each st around. (10 sc)

Round 4: [Inv-dec] 2 times, sc in next 6 sts. (8 sc)

Round 5: Sc in each st around. (8 sc)

Fasten off, leaving a tail for sewing.

Stuff lightly.

FINAL ASSEMBLY

1. Sew Body onto the Head. *(Image 13)*

2. Sew Bowtie onto the Body. *(Image 14)*

3. Sew Arms onto the Body. *(Image 15)*

4. Sew Legs onto the lower part of the Body. *(Image 16)*

5. All done! *(Images 17 & 18)*

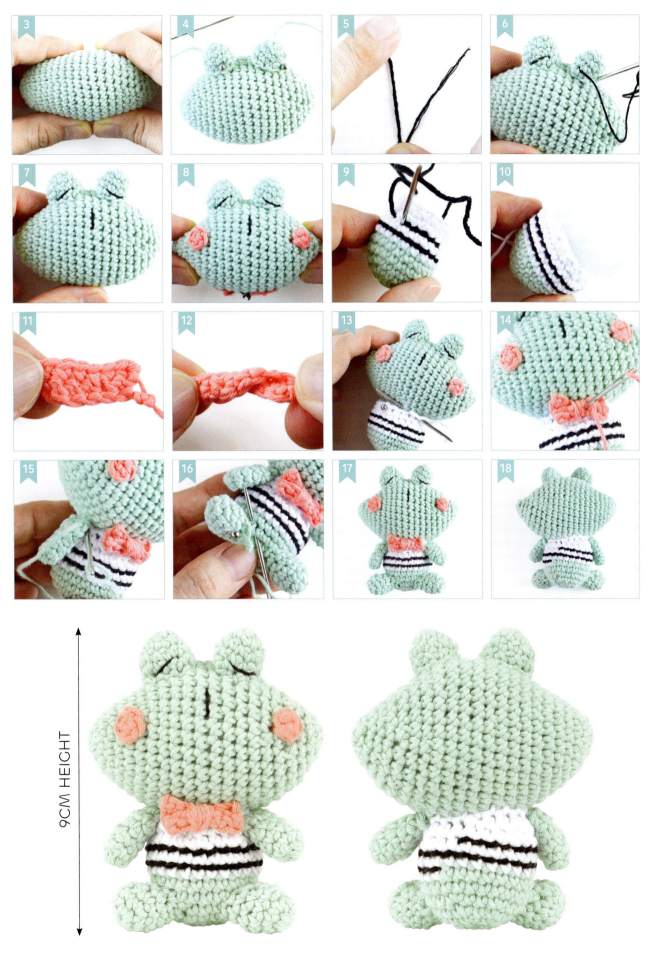

9CM HEIGHT

Skill Level

Easy

WESLEY THE WHALE

This little baby whale likes to pretend that he is a sailor of the seven seas!

Finished Size: About 3" (8 cm) tall

MATERIALS & TOOLS

HELLO COTTON YARN

- **Main colour (MC):** Blue (148) - Body, Tail and Stripes on Hat
- **Colour A:** White (154) - Body and Hat
- **Colour B:** Black (160) - Eyes and Lips
- **Colour C:** Light Pink (102) - Blush

HOOK SIZE
2.5 mm hook

OTHER
Toy Stuffing
Tapestry Needle
Stitch Marker

BODY

Round 1: With MC, make a magic ring, 6 sc in ring. (6 sc)
Round 2: Inc in each st around. (12 sc)
Round 3: [Sc in next st, inc] 6 times. (18 sc)
Round 4: [Sc in next 2 sts, inc] 6 times. (24 sc)
Round 5: [Sc in next 3 sts, inc] 6 times. (30 sc)
Round 6: [Sc in next 4 sts, inc] 6 times. (36 sc)
Round 7: [Sc in next 5 sts, inc] 6 times. (42 sc)
Round 8: [Sc in next 6 sts, inc] 6 times. (48 sc)
Rounds 9-15: *(7 rounds)* Sc in each st around. (48 sc)
Rounds 16-17: *(2 rounds)* Change to Color A. Sc in each st around. (48 sc) *(Image 1)*
Round 18: [Sc in next 6 sts, inv-dec] 6 times. (42 sc)
Round 19: [Sc in next 5 sts, inv-dec] 6 times. (36 sc)
Round 20: [Sc in next 4 sts, inv-dec] 6 times. (30 sc)
Round 21: [Sc in next 3 sts, inv-dec] 6 times. (24 sc)
Round 22: [Sc in next 2 sts, inv-dec] 6 times. (18 sc) *(Image 2)*
Start stuffing Body, adding more as you go. *(Image 3)*
At this point, gently use your hands to squeeze and re-shape the Body to give it an oval-like appearance (when viewed from the top). *(Images 4 & 5)*
Round 23: [Sc in next st, inv-dec] 6 times. (12 sc)
Round 24: [Inv-dec] 6 times. (6 sc)
Fasten off and close the opening securely. *(Image 6)*

BLUSH (Make 2)

Round 1: With Color C, make a magic ring, 5 sc in ring. (5 sc) Fasten off and leave a tail for sewing.

DESIGNING THE FACE

Lips

1. To sew the Lips, you will need to split Color B up to thinner strands. *(Image 7)*

93

2. Take 5 of the strands and make a horizontal Back Stitch (9-stitches-long) at the bottom of Round 17, centered on the shorter end of the body. To find this position, make sure that the longer/wider part of the Body piece is facing the sides. *(Image 8)*

Closed Eyelids

1. With the same 5 strands of Color B, sew on a "V" shape (across 3 stitches) for each Closed Eyelids on Round 15, positioned near both ends of the Lips. *(Images 9 & 10)*

2. Knot ends and hide inside the Body.

Blush

Sew on Blush pieces below each Eyelid. *(Image 11)*

HAT

Round 1: With Color A, make a magic ring, 6 sc in ring. (6 sc)

Round 2: Inc in each st around. (12 sc)

Rounds 3-5: *(3 rounds)* Sc in each st around. (12 sc)

Round 6: In **front loops** only, [sc in next st, inc] 6 times. (18 sc)

Round 7: [Sc in next 2 sts, inc] 6 times. (24 sc)

Round 8: Sc in each st around. (24 sc) Fasten off and leave a long tail for sewing. Fold up the brim.

HAT DETAIL

- Using MC and your tapestry needle, embroider small Back Stitches all around the bottom of Round 3 of the Hat. *(Image 12)*
- Stuff Hat.

TAIL (Make 2)

Round 1: With MC, make a magic ring, 3 sc in ring. (3 sc)

Round 2: Inc in each st around. (6 sc)

Round 3: [Sc in next st, inc] 3 times. (9 sc)

Rounds 4-5: *(2 rounds)* Sc in each st around. (9 sc)

Round 6: [Sc in next st, inv-dec] 3 times. (6 sc) Don't stuff Tail. Fasten off and leave a tail for sewing. Flatten piece.

FINAL ASSEMBLY

1. Sew Hat to the top of the Body. Make it slanted and leaning towards one of the Eyelids. *(Image 13)*

2. Sew on the Tail pieces at the back of the Body, on Round 16 and 17, one above the other. *(Image 14)*

3. Pinch the tails to give them more shape, so that they look like the letter "C" from the side. *(Image 15)*

4. And you're all done! *(Image 16)*